T5-ARO-538

Why won't they listen to me?

**How to influence your
pack and move them in the
direction you want them to go**

Dr. Janet Lapp

DEMETER PRESS

NEW YORK

Library of Congress Publisher's Cataloging In Publication Data
Lapp, Janet E.
            Why Won't They Listen to Me?
            Janet E. Lapp
                    p.cm.
            ISBN 1-885365-34-9
1. Leadership
2. Psychology - Parenting
            I.Title   II. Title:
BF637.S4S24 2009
158' . 1-dc20

Cartoon reprint permissions received.

CHAPTER OUTLINE

Introduction

No matter how bad things have become, they can always improve and be healed. That is a testimony to the power of the human spirit. But things don't get better on their own. Separating and giving distance won't make it better. The only way beyond it is through it. Winston Churchill once said, "If you're going through hell, keep going."

If you are resentful, it means that you have given up your power and decision-making ability, given someone else responsibility, and let him or her do as they wish with you. You feel victimized and hurt, and are mad at the other person for treating you this way. You demand that he or she change to suit you, rather than speaking up and taking responsibility for yourself. This is a very immature way of handling life, one which you used years ago as a child when you had no choice. It no longer is working for you, and it is time to give it up, and grow up.

No matter how out of control things have become, none of it was your fault. You didn't know. You didn't ask to not know how to lead a pack. You didn't understand how to take power; you weren't shown how to do it.

Reading this book shows you care about making things better, not only for your current relationships but for the next generation. When you have finished the book, you will at last have a road map to make that happen.

Quick Start:

What to change now

You want solutions quickly, without wading through much theory and explanation first[1]. Your interactions will improve if you follow the advice in the Quick Start section, but you will feel more confident and knowledgeable if you read the whole book.

After the Quick-Start section, read Changing the System (Chapter 4), and the 5C's (Chapters 6-8). Then later hit Chapters 1-3. I felt a responsibility to put causation and focus on what's wrong in Chapters 1-3, but you can go directly to Chapters 4-9 because they are immediately helpful.

All the research (of which I'm aware) on why people listen to other people, is condensed for you here. Read it,

---

1 *Many years ago when I learned how to fly an airplane, I just wanted to get up there and chase around the clouds. About ten years ago, I got around to studying and understanding the engine. Did my lack of understanding limit the joy of flying? Not really. But now I feel safer and more confident, know what I am doing, and why I'm doing it. It's more fun knowing why. I think it works the same way with human systems.

and follow the suggestions if you really want things to improve. Then, you can read the rest of the book if you want to understand how things got this way, or want to delve deeper into some of the psychological issues.

Continuing the way you are now will continue to yield the results you are currently getting. Perhaps you are waiting for something or someone else to make changes, but it doesn't work that way. Others won't change to suit you, they'll change to suit themselves.

You have three choices in changing the situation. Those are:
__ 1. Change the other person
__ 2. Change the situation
__ 3. Change yourself

Let's face it. You've been mad at the person or people who've been resisting you, right? If that's true, then the underlying expectation is that they should do the changing and if they did, things would just work better. Not that you're controlling, but if they did it your way, it would work better. You know, after all. Don't be offended (or if you are, please don't leave).

Expecting the other person to change, or waiting until the situation magically changes, is fairy-tale thinking. Only by getting over your resentment and realizing that you are the part of the equation that needs to change, is there hope that things will change as in: "You spot it, you got it."

© Mark Parisi. Cartoon printed with permission.

SEVEN QUICK-STARTS

Here's the research. People will listen to what you say, if you have any, or some of the qualities listed, numbered from the least difficult to change to the hardest to change. Note they are not listed in their degree of effectiveness; that depends on each situation.

QUICK-START #1

___ You have information that is interesting, valuable, important or useful to them (not you, them)

Did you do your research and find out what would motivate the other person? People do things for their own reasons, not for yours. They'll resist watching the slides from your summer vacation, but they can't wait to show you theirs. That's just human nature.

QUICK-START #2
___ You are able to bond others to you.

People will listen when they feel listened to. People will bond to you not only if you listen to them, but if you make them feel special and unique. Self-esteem, or feeling-good-about-self, rises if one feels listened to. So others will feel good about you and bond to you insofar as they feel good about themselves when they are with you.

People also become absorbed and more easily influenced by an absorbing and relevant story or parable. Dig through *Readers Digest* or Google your area of interest to come up with stories or short parables if you don't have any of your own. Keep your short stories short –maybe one or three minutes maximum. Stories and parables have been known to be engaging and hypnotic since the early Greeks, so they should work for you too.

QUICK-START #3
___ You use the right qualifiers

Those who tend to be ignored, often ask to be ignored. They qualify their statements by saying things like "This might not make sense, but ..." I just wanted to add that ..."

Those who get listened to add powerful qualifiers such as "This is absolutely amazing, listen to this ..." "You've got to hear this!" Ask for what you want.

QUICK-START #4
___ You have credibility

It helps if you have position or influence, or can get it. If you are a parent and have lost credibility, you've lost it. Pulling power by saying, "I'm your father, that's why!" is a joke. You can gain credibility by third-party endorsements; in business, create positive rumors about yourself (have others spread information that increases your credibility) or if a parent, have a third source reinforce you as a credible leader.

QUICK-START #5

____ You have charisma ... a good voice, animated presence, entertaining, make a strong impression

You can learn how to present yourself more effectively and become more entertaining. Your choice.

QUICK-START #6

____ You have wealth, power, beauty or fame

This is the basis for celebrity endorsements. For better or worse, research shows that we listen to, and are influenced by, those with those qualities listed above. Was Schwarzenegger brought into John McCain's campaign because of the role he played as California's governor? Was Al Gore brought into President Obama's campaign because of his role as the 2000 Democratic candidate? No.

QUICK-START #7

____ You are a friend, relative, or acquaintance
"Birds of a feather flock together." The influence of MySpace and Facebook derive from the communities that have been established. Members of those sites feel they are friends ... part of the same community, and thence are trustworthy. This variable is the business basis for joining network groups; friends or acquaintances are more likely to be able to influence you.

Let's get more specific and talk about changes you can quick-start now. There are five main variables involved in influencing others. These are covered in more depth later in the book, but here's a summary for you quick-start folks:

#1: Compassion (page 108)

How you listen to others dictates how they feel about themselves. How they feel about themselves dictates how much they will like you, and thus listen to what you might have to say.

"It's easy to love the lovable.
The challenge is to love the unlovable."

1. Get into The Other Person's World
2. Be Likable :-) The highest form of love, in the Greek
        language, means "look for the good"
a. Praise in specifics.
b. Praise successes and efforts.
c. Stop negative comments and judging. Next time, don't
        react. Stop.

#2 Confidence (page 123)

a. The degree to which others will follow you will depend on your confidence in being their leader. Work on your visible confidence (your tone, posture, words) first, and your underlying confidence will follow. Don't wait for confidence to increase; it only increases by your actions, it won't increase on it's own. If you are not sure of what you want or in your ability to reinforce it, you will be easily manipulated.

b. Whatever is given energy, increases. That is, when you get mad at another's behavior, you are increasing the chances that the other person's behavior will happen again, and probably increase.

1. Develop the Calm-Assertive energy of pack leaders

Stop saying powerless, ineffectual comments such as:

"she annoys me"   "they drive me nuts"

"he is inconsiderate"   "she is making me crazy"

"these kids are driving me insane."

Those comments give power to the other person (not a leader position), feed into your victim status (not a leader position), and indicate resentment or negative energy toward the other person (not a leader position).

2. Develop Your Own Identity

If you are not sure of what you want, or in your ability to reinforce it, you will be easily manipulated.

3. Communicate Confidence
What is your nonverbal behavior communicating?

Tone, pitch, and pacing.

Eye contact

Posture open

Natural gestures–no pointing, banging, tapping

Speak clearly, not too fast. Don't yell!

Neutral, slightly positive face

Face directly

Distance appropriate

Move inwards, and nod agreement

Balance, no feet shifting

#3 Clarity - Get Clear (page 130)

1. Listen! Before an impulse reaction ...
a. Restate what you heard
>"So you believe..."   "You want to ..."
b. Reflect on what's going on at a deeper level.
>Ask yourself: "How would I be feeling"?
c. Question the other person using open-ended questions:
>"Can you tell me more about that?"

2. Be direct and clear
a. Stop saying things like:
>"We" as in "We need-to" "Somebody has to"
>"You" as in "Why don't you?" "You'll have
>to ..." or "... You need to ..."
b. Get out of False Power: "You do it this minute or ..."
c. Be simple. Dumb it Down.
d. Ask in the Positive Future: "I would like you to ..."

3. Correct Others Behavior Clearly and Concisely
1. Recognize

>"I can see that you want to stay out later"
2. State limit calmly/clearly

13

"We agreed on 8:00 p.m., and will stick to that."

3. Point out ways for partial fulfillment of their wishes

"Perhaps Joan can visit at our place tomorrow."

4. Help express natural resentment

"You might be upset, that's understandable."

Example:

1. "When you throw your glass (describe)

2. It breaks things (explain why it's important)

3. That is not OK, and can't happen (consequence)

4. So, when you are mad, instead of throwing your glass, use words to say you are angry and say what you want. Then I won't need to cancel your friend's visit" (what needs to happen).

#4 Commitment (page 143)

Get Real. Commit to your Commitments. If you aren't really committed to the issues you say you are, and then you try to enforce them in other's lives, they just won't stick. Not credible. Hypocritical, even.

Make a list of your most important commitments, and rank them from most important to least important. Start with the top five. How much time and money do you spend on each of them? Are these evident in your life? If no, or not much, increase time and energy on them, or let them go as commitments. Maybe you will have a separate list of the areas in which others don't listen to you, and then observe your own behavior in these areas. You might list things such as neatness, telling the truth, high marks in school, healthy eating, drug or alcohol use, losing weight, not playing funky music so loud, exercising, spiritual practice and so on.

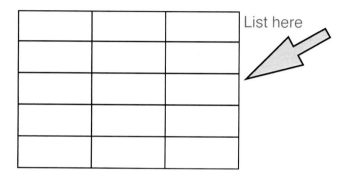

List here

#5 Consistency (page 146)

a. If you give in once, they've got you.

b. Don't make promises you can't keep. Don't make threats in anger that you'll regret later.

c. Expect manipulations:

THEM   "But I'll have no friends"
YOU   "That might be true, but you won't be going tonight."
THEM   "But I'll fail in school if I don't go!"
YOU   "That might be true, but you won't be going tonight."
THEM   "You are so mean!"
YOU   "That might be true, but you won't be going tonight."
THEM   "I hate you so much!"
YOU   "That might be true, but you're not going tonight."
THEM   "You bitch!" (slam door)
YOU   Silence. Deep breath. You're doing fine.

Consistency Guidelines:

1. Don't get upset. It's not about you.

2. Don't reject the manipulator, it's not her fault.

3. Trust your gut, always. If in doubt that you are being manipulated, buy time, get help.

4. Be patient. Change doesn't happen when we want it. It happens for it's own reason.

5. No tit-for-tat. Don't play their game, they will win.

6. Love your enemies. It drives them nuts.

7. Figure out what you want and what you'll settle for, in advance.

8. Identify their tactics to them.

9. Change timing, it derails their efforts.

> Pause: say nothing and buy time.
>
> Review: "Let me understand"
>
> Take time Out.
>
> Disarm by surprise: Do the opposite of what's expected.

10. Don't give up. Don't give in and settle for less than you know what is right.

Chapter One:
Why Aren't They Listening?

"It started innocently enough. My eleven-year-old knew she was supposed to turn off the TV right after High School Musical. She knew that. It was an agreement we had; but at the end of the program, when I reminded her to turn it off, she said, "Oh mom, this is a cool commercial, look at these dogs. I just want to watch this, and then I'll turn it off." So I figured one commercial doesn't hurt, and she does love dogs.

Somehow I got busy, and didn't notice that the next program had begun. I was kind of upset, and I went in and told her that she promised that she would turn it off after the commercial, and she said, "Mom, I didn't know this special was on, this is on gymnastics–how to enter competitions and how to choose coaches. Oh-my-gawd it is JUST what I need to know. Just this one program, and I *promise* I will go right to sleep! I always read before bed anyway, and I won't read tonight so it will be the same

17

thing, I will still get to sleep at 10:00 PM so there's no difference."

I felt torn, because I had told her to turn it off, and she had promised, but I did want her to get interested in gymnastics and thought maybe if she watched it, it would spark her interest. If we had TIVO we could have recorded it, but we don't. After all, what would it hurt if she got to sleep at the same time, I could see her point of view. So I agreed to watch to the end of the show, and during the commercials to go brush her teeth and get ready for bed. That she did, so I felt pretty good even though I was kind of resentful underneath that she got her own way again.

I guess I lost it when the commercials started after the gymnastics show, and she still wasn't turning it off. By then I couldn't believe she wasn't turning it off. So I went in, and I guess I yelled: "I told you to turn it off and you promised. I cannot believe you are like this! You are always getting your way, you are always pushing me to the limit. You get upstairs this minute, and you know what? No more TV for you for a month. You are so self-centered; it is always about what *you* want."

Why doesn't she listen to me? Why doesn't she do what I ask the first time, why do we always go around and around like this? What is the matter with her?

Cartoon printed with permission.

We could repeat the same scenario in situations at work, in relationships, wherever two or more people are interacting. The dynamics are the same, the actors differ. Why do we still not get it? There has been so much written, and so many guidelines published, on how to communicate well, how to parent effectively–and at last count there were 14,320 published leadership books. What has been missing is the basic idea of the Pack Leader, one that has been popularized by the Dog Whisperer Cesar Milan[2] and now the subject of increasing attention, and I have a confession to make: you would know everything needed to know if you read and followed the alpha guidelines from C.A.R.E.S. in the Appendix on page 177.

---

2 Cesar's Way: The Natural Everyday Guide to Understanding and Correcting Common Dog Problems and his 2007 book Be the Pack Leader. His show 'Dog Whisperer' airs on the National Geographic Channel Fridays 8:00pm ET/PT

However, this is a book that translates some of these commonsense principles from the animal to the human world—one that I wish that I had read, and guidelines followed, before raising my own children. I write it not only for myself, but for those like me who are educated enough to know better, care but don't always show it in the right way; want the best for their kids, and still don't get what's wrong. Like most parents, I meant well and cared deeply too, but could have avoided misunderstandings, problems with respect and boundaries, and resentments if I had simply adjusted a few things. It's all doable, have hope!

> *We took our Lhasa Apso, Muffin, to Obedience Classes, but did not know how to establish a household where the adults are alpha. We all wanted Muffin to be a free, loving, fully expressed and happy dog, so as long as she wasn't destroying anything and went potty outdoors, we thought we were doing well. She slept on our beds, sat in our chairs, sat up front in the car, ate first, went out the door first, and was a full member of our family. It wasn't until she was about five years old that she started growling when anyone approached the bed she was guarding. It wasn't until she was eight years old that she started biting when she was approached by strangers. In the era before Cesar Milan and the Dog Whisperer, there were no animal behaviorists who said she could be treated.*

How the Pack (Family) Works

The two dominant (alpha) wolves silently part company, the alpha female circling around front, blocking exit, and the alpha male running up behind. The alpha male quickly takes down the gazelle, and two juveniles rush in to participate. The alphas eat first, then the juveniles, and only later

the non-dominant members of the pack. The pack is efficient, cooperative. The Alpha leads a flawless hunt. After the kill, he or she monitors the order of feeding. He and his mate eat first; then they allow their offspring to join in. Subordinates wait, knowing there will be lots left for them. The alpha is not being cruel; he or she is communicating order and system. He is the leader of the pack; the others in the pack feel secure.

A wolf pack is a highly disciplined and efficient group. All members know their ranking and (usually) accept this naturally. The most essential element in the survival of the group is the establishment of a system of order, established through pack hierarchy. The pack order defines relationships in the group, and controls and directs the behavior of the members.

In the pack order, the leader is always respected by pack members. He sets the rules, initiates the hunt, motivates the pack, protects, and disciplines. To preserve status, the Alpha keeps asserting his position; he eats first, sleeps highest, controls space, and initiates interactions. If a subordinate male challenges the leadership position, the pack will become unstable. A pack with stable leadership maintains itself and raises its healthy juveniles to maturity.

There is no difference in how wolves relate to their pack leaders and how your child relates to, and determines its ranking, in your pack. Parents who placate their children and make them the center of attention, communicate to their children that they are dominant. As far as children are concerned, only leaders would be treated in the way that they are being treated, so they are forced into exerting authority, always with immaturity.

When parents treat children democratically, allowing them to determine their own actions, they are unknowingly teaching them that they are the leaders. When children are the leaders of their packs, they have the right and responsibility to discipline members of their pack. So they do. Witness the tantrum your child is throwing on the supermarket floor.

Now, think of your child(ren). Are any of these true?

Do you meet her needs first, before yours (infants excepted)?

Does she have a tantrum when she doesn't get her own way?

Does he refuse to share his toys with others?

Does your child determine where you eat lunch, against your better judgment?

Does your child go through doors ahead of you?

Does your teen talk back to you?

Does your child sleep in bed with you?

Does your teen pester you until you give in?

Do you always let your child win when playing games?

Does your child want to run around a store, and protests walking beside you, or sitting in the basket?

Does your child put up a fight when it's time to go to bed?

Must you repeat requests to get your child to listen?

Does your teenager steal your things or take loose change hanging around?

None of those sentences should be endorsed. *Not one.* If you found you indicated yes to any of the above statements, you're in the right place. Okay, let's run through some tough ideas I want you to think about:

1. Difference between Discipline and Punishment

When I refer to discipline in this book, it is very far removed from the idea of punishment. Discipline is just order, much like how a wolf pack and the

23

way all of nature works, and thus the way human relationships need to work too. Through discipline, all species remain healthy and fed, and can survive until the next generation takes over. It is the natural order of things. Discipline is necessary for a child's health. Discipline is not punitive, it is just the requirement to follow the rules of the pack.

Although there is a role for punishment in leading others, punishment should be used sparingly and carefully if at all; its effects are not permanent, and it inevitably produces other, unwanted side effects such as anxiety. Above all, if punishment is used, it must be used without anger, it must be thought out in advance, and be predictable and understandable. If it isn't, the child's world becomes chaotic and unpredictable ... but more about that later. When playtime is over in the puppy world, the canine elders gently nose their pups to the ground, maybe with a gentle bite, a pickup by the neck, and in rare instances, a growl. They indicate that playtime is over only once, and the pups obey. The human world should operate in the same way.

2. Where to Look for the Answer: You Can't Hide
Whenever there is a dysfunction in a child, there is always a dysfunction in another part of the family system. Kids don't get out of whack all by themselves, out of nowhere.

That's why we rarely if ever treat a child alone, but only in the context of the family system.

Your kids sense how you feel. They know what is lying beneath the surface, even if you don't. They closely watch your nonverbal behavior, listen attentively to your words, and respond accordingly. Their very survival depends on them understanding your system, so they can't get it wrong. When there is a mismatch between your nonverbal language and your words, their small world is thrown into chaos and they don't have the skills to call you on the discrepancies. If there is inconsistency in your words and actions, it is crazy-making for their small world.

A more important point is this: kids will pick up and act out the underlying pack feeling tone. Is a child depressed? Let's look for unexpressed depression in the adults. How about defiant? Seething with anger? Where is the unexpressed anger lingering–how do we get at it, expose it, and let the kid off the hook? Kids often carry their parents' emotions for them, a difficult idea for most parents to get, because these emotions are unexpressed and sometimes even pushed out of awareness so far, that they are not even felt.

> *"My daughter would start to yell, 'Don't be angry, mommy, don't be angry, please don't be angry. Say you're sorry, say you're sorry!' and I had no idea what she was*

> *talking about, and it would annoy me after a while. 'What do you mean angry? Sorry? Stop it! I **will** get angry if you keep that up, I am NOT angry!' I was so unconscious about all this, and it wasn't until about 20 years later that I started to uncover all the latent anger that I had stored up and frozen away. I never felt angry, I never expressed anger. It just wasn't anything I could bring myself to do. So she was just expressing something inside me, poor kid, something she couldn't understand or explain–because it wasn't hers!"*

This system requires that you see your part in the interaction only, not the other party's response. Your job will be to keep your side of the street clean, not to worry about the mess on the other person's sidewalk. Thus, the system guides you into taking increasing responsibility for your influencing skills, and less and less concern (and resentment) about how the other person is responding.

3. Understand the Power of Reinforcement

Reinforcement is an immediate increase in the strength of a response following a change in a reinforcer. What is a reinforcer to one person, may not be a reinforcer to another person. If a child gets a chocolate bar when he or she asks for one, and the frequency of 'chocolate bar-requesting behavior' increases; the chocolate bar is reinforcing 'chocolate bar-requesting behavior'. If chocolate bar-requesting behavior does not go up, the chocolate bar is not reinforcing. We watch the change in the behavior after giving the reinforcer.

Positive reinforcement is an increase in the future frequency of a behavior due to a reinforcer being given immediately following a response. Giving (or *adding*) food to a dog if it sits is an example of positive reinforcement (if it results in an increase in the future behavior of the dog sitting).

© Mark Parisi. Cartoon printed with permission.

Negative reinforcement is an increase in the future frequency of a behavior when something bad is turned off or taken away. For example, your kid is screaming in the drug store. You offer a package of M&M's to turn it off. It works, and she stops screaming. She has just used a negative reinforcer on you to control your behavior. Whenever she stops screaming, you give her M&M's because it worked in the past. Your teenage son nags you about the car, you have already said no a dozen times, but he won't stop. He has this nasal high-pitched whine he uses when he pesters you, and you hate it. Just to shut him up, you say, "Fine! Go take the damn car ... just leave me alone." You have given him a positive reinforcement for his nasal, high-pitched whine, making it more likely for him the use it in the future, and he has used negative reinforcement on you, turning off the aversive whining and making it more likely that you will give in, in the future. What a great system these mutual reinforcers are.

Pay very careful attention to the reinforcement system that you have inadvertently set up. To a child who might not be getting enough attention from you, your anger is a powerful reinforcer, and she will naturally do the things that create your anger. If a child gets the most nurturing affection and attention when he is sick, and not at other times, the chances are that his sickness will increase. The

	UNKIND	KIND	
		you are here	NOT FIRM
		it works better here	FIRM

focus of this book, then, will be on reordering the pack hierarchy, using appropriate reinforcement and getting discipline in order.

Why Aren't They Listening to You?

If your kids (or employees) aren't listening to you, it just means that your position in the box below needs to be shuffled downwards. It's that easy. The goal of this book is to nudge you down–and you can do it once you realize what's going on and what to do about it. Kids can move out of unstable behavior quickly if we let them.

The very fact that you have opened this book tells me that you are kind, willing, motivated, and have what it takes to do it. You will find things easier if you are starting this before your child hits the teen years, because the window of opportunity starts to close around the age of 12-13 years. However, even after that time–with your courage and persistence and everyone on board–turnarounds are possible. If you are reading this book to help you develop authority and control with employees, the same principles apply. The earlier you start this program, the easier it is.

Consequences

At the mild end of problems, the parent–governing authority–pack leader simply has lost authority and control. To take up the slack, inexperienced and unprepared pack members (kids, employees), have started to exert authority in an unskilled way. The unprepared pack leader uses everything but real leadership power to try to regain control. Some of the reactions of unskilled parents include resentment, occasional blowups, emotional withdrawal, inconsistent discipline, giving up, and the general complaint: "Why won't they listen to me?" At the extreme end, this well-meaning yet ineffective parenting can lead to defiant kids, conduct disorders and sociopathies. Regardless, your own issues are mirrored in your kids' behaviors. Their acting out is a gift to you so that you can see and correct what's going on with you. Great, eh? :-) Children expect order, they want calm, they naturally want to follow rules and they want their parents to be the leaders.

Instead of learning how to be happy, the kids described in this book learn to expect more fun, and continued support from their parents, and eventually have the same expectations of life. "Someone will come along and rescue me, discover me, and make it all right. I should get what I want, now." The secret wish of every parent or leader described in this book is that their kids will react to their efforts with "Whew, this is cool! I love, adore and appreciate my parents!" Why do kids react with entitlement and resentment when all you want for them is the best? All this confuses parents, who have only given to their kids. They expect happiness in their kids, and they get this!

What kind of parents are we describing in this book? Well-meaning and often very educated and sophisticated people, who are either short on skills, emotionally out of shape, harboring guilt, have negative self-images, and/or have problems with rejection and fear of loss of approval. If you are reading this, chances are you are in that group. Before you put the book down in defiance, read the next sentence. Has what you have been doing so far been working?

You've tried everything you know. That means that what will help is something that you DON'T know. What is keeping you from knowing what you don't know, is the reaction you just had to reading about what might be wrong? It is called resistance, denial, fear ... whatever ... you've got it. You might want to believe that you don't need to change anything about yourself, and that someone else will recognize how unfair it is that you have had to deal with a child (or an employee) who is so difficult. Well, the bad news is that that won't happen. The good news is that you have a chance at breaking through it right now. Don't live a half-life the rest of your life, and raise your child to be less than he or she could, because of fear. Just read the book and do what it suggests.

Why People Don't Listen

Why *would* people listen to you?

People do things for two reasons, a) because they want to, and b) because they have to. Your job is to get people to *want* to do what you want them to do, because if they are doing it only because they have to do it, they will do it only when you are standing behind them with a threat held over their heads.

People will listen to your point-of-view and change over to what you want them to do when the fear of changing (doing what you want) is less than the pain of staying the same, or, the reward to doing it your way is greater than the reward of doing it their way, and they see it that way. They will quit smoking when they get that the consequences of smoking (as they understand them) are just too much greater than the consequences of quitting.

Re-Think Resistance.

There is an oriental saying: "If a medium in which you wish to create offers no resistance, there can be no durable impression." If you put your finger in a bowl of water, then in ball of clay, only one gives you permanent change. Kids resist parents, students resist teachers, employees resist employers, prospects resist salespeople, marriage partners resist each other. That is the gist of human interaction. Expecting that there would be no resistance is creating a false universe of expectation that is doomed to fail. It just isn't the real world.

Try looking at resistance as interesting. It is intriguing. Do not look at resistance as a threat. Don't react emotionally. It is not a threat. It is just resistance. Resistance is good for the one who is resisting you. Because he or she is resisting you, you have a chance to learn about yourself. If everyone in your life agreed with you, and did it your way, you'd learn nothing and never grow. The person resisting you is showing a level of mental health, and developing some strength as an added bonus, and this is good. Resistance helps develop determination, backbone, purpose, resolution, and will power. When your two-year-old daughter (or 14-year-old son or 36-year-old spouse) is resisting you, they're getting stronger. That is exactly what they are supposed to be doing.

Children resist parents, students resist teachers, employees resist employers, prospects resist salespeople, marriage partners resist each other. So, somebody isn't doing what you want, and you feel frustrated, anxious, irritated, blocked, resentful. You want this something from somebody else, and get frustrated when you don't get it. What happens normally, is that you punish the other person to get what you want. How is *that* supposed to work? How successful you are in changing your system depends on you changing your attitude toward resistance in the first place.

Let's look at resistance for a bit longer because if you, as a parent, expect no resistance from your child, you have more reading to do! Your two-year-old says, "No" and you take it as a declaration of war. "What do you mean saying no to me who do you think I am young man you get right over here this minute when I'm talking to you!" Like you get all into power ... this anger just builds resistance. Give it up. Your attitude toward resistance will determine how successful you are in dealing with it.

Stop getting mad at resistance! We get frustrated (mild form of anger) because it's the only way we can feel any power over it. Mad just makes worse.

Physically, the universe works because of resistance. Your muscles develop strength as they resist weights. Don't get all tied up in knots because people are not doing what you want. Being tied-up-in-knots is part of the problem, and when you learn to relax around this stuff, it will work better and you'll be more effective.

Nothing you do will be effective if it's covering up sarcasm, exasperation, ridicule, revenge, or disrespect. What is needed is to redevelop an underlying compassion or understanding; that happens in Chapter Six.

An effective pack leader is calm and assertive. A leader who is emitting the negative energy of the emotions listed above, will create a response in followers of anxiety, aggression, anger, complaining, foot dragging, frustration and depression–sound familiar? These emotions can, as mentioned earlier, turn into more severe depressive or anxiety disorders, school problems, conduct disorders and criminal behaviors, so they are worth cutting them out early. At work, they can lead to sabotage, illness, accidents, absenteeism, and turnover. That said, chances are you still hate or resent the person or situation that's resisting you.

If getting mad gives you artificial power, it means you don't have enough natural power. Anger seems to give you power, but it removes your potential for real power. If you were confident, you wouldn't need anger.

The basic goal is this book is to help you develop enough determination, consistency, backbone, clarity, purpose, resolution, compassion, will power, and freedom so that you will be able to lead your pack in the direction you want and need them to go in a natural, calm and assertive manner.

Whoever loses control, loses the interaction. If you are dominated by emotions, you place yourself lower in the hierarchy of power, giving the other party automatic dominance over you. Whatever behavior put you in that uncontrolled emotional position will be repeated. Honor the resistance. Be at peace with what is going on now. I can hear you muttering: "Yeah, right!" Yeah right.

Maybe you can let it go.

When parents talk to me about their teenagers who won't listen, they are often describing a fairly 'normal' range of behaviors, but ones that don't fit their fairly narrow standards of how teenagers should act. Anger, complaining, foot dragging, frustration and depression are all natural, and probably will pass if well managed. If not well managed, of course, these can turn into sabotage, illness, school failures, accidents, and suicide attempts. Before we go on, what isn't being listened to? If it is minor and it should be outside your control, is it worth the energy? Sometimes you can just let it go.

Supposing your 12-year-old son is compliant in every other way than cleaning his room. What if your daughter is a model child other than insisting on wearing her hair short, with bangs covering her forehead ... let it go! Your husband has only one thing that really annoys you–his weight. His diet is terrible, and he resists exercise. No matter what you say or do, he doesn't listen. Let it go. Let it go! Back off. Your nagging him is only making him more resistant. He will change it when he wants to, in his way–or he won't. He might never change it, and yes he might die an earlier death than he would if he were to lose the weight, and maybe you feel that that isn't fair–but it is not your life, your path, it is his, get the point?

If your child's behavior is compliant about 85-90% of the time, and the area he is resisting is really not that central to his development, let it go. If the resistance is considerably more important ... such as truancy at school, lying, stealing, talking back constantly, ignoring your

37

rules and guidelines ... then now is a good time to apply the principles you will learn in this book.

The overall goals of your book are to:

a.   Help you get rid of your underlying frustration, because people around you sense it and will resist. Then, to help you develop a calm assertive style of leadership.

b.   Change your current reactions to resistance.

c.   Show others what they need to do to learn new behaviors.

We often spend way too much time trying to figure out why the other person isn't listening to us ... what is wrong with her, anyway? ... rather than working on being more effective as influencers.

"God grant me the serenity to accept the things I cannot change the courage to change the things I can, and the wisdom to know the difference."
Reinhold Niebuhr

Chapter Two:
The Quick Fix

A child expects, and thrives with, order. Kids in packs
expect to work for food, follow the rules and guidelines.
Not understanding the orderly work-for-food idea, and
expecting and needing constant gratification, you will find
them sulking, whining, having tantrums (very unskilled
behaviors) when they don't get that gratification, in an
attempt to lead the pack. These sulking, whining, and
tantrum behaviors are mini-models of eating disorders
and impulsive disorders that you'll see popping up in their
late teens.

**If kids get stuff randomly, independent of
anything they are doing to deserve it, they just
don't develop motivation. Why should they?
Stuff comes anyway.**

'Stuff coming anyway' is what I call a **Quick Fix**. Kids
stop listening because they are going to get fixed whether

they listen or not. Healthy pack members rely on a pack leader that has predictability, authority and control, to be fed. So those pack members listen up; they know it won't work out if they do it their way.

Why do parents fail to develop that clean, orderly system and rely on the quick fixes? The parents we find most often producing quick-fix-kids-who-don't-listen are busy, distracted parents. What distracts them might vary from getting their own needs met, addictions to work or chemicals, or just an unconscious repetition of poor pack leadership skills. Regardless, the solution is the same for all. To understand the notion of quick-fixes and to (perhaps) recognize them in yourself, the following section describes varieties of the quick-fix. Don't be discouraged or depressed reading this; got to go through the painful recognition stage before getting into the illumination stage. As Winston Churchill once said, "If you're going through hell, keep going."

#1 The Rescuing Quick Fix

A child finally receives a consequence for his behavior (hooray) but the parent tries to eliminate the consequence the child earned. For example, a child is sent to a time-out location and mom brings in sandwiches and a favorite drink. A junior in high school is always late, to the point of disciplinary action by the school. Since there is no parking near the school, the parents sell their home in the adjacent neighborhood and buy a home two blocks from the school so their son can get to school on time. That kind of thing.

It is not unusual that most parents want to be heroes in their children's lives. Quick-Fix parents achieve false hero status, by rescuing their children from earned consequences they deserve. They receive a quick-fix from their children, who inflate the parents when they in turn, have provided a quick-fix rescue. "Oh mommy thank you! You are the absolute best mommy in the whole world! I love you so much!" This lasts for a few minutes, but is so reinforcing to the parent that it's good enough.

#2 Quick-Fix Praise

Quick-Fix kids often hear glowing comments from their parents, without the balance of instruction about things they need to correct. Lavished emotional praise that is tied to the parent's needs instead of the child's is damaging. For a parent to pay attention to whatever needs to be corrected in their kids, they have to first see it, and then spend the time and energy to set up an  informal teaching program for their kids. It takes time and energy to pay attention to what the kid is doing, what she is attempting, how she is growing, and to reinforce it. Quick-Fix Kids never hear this from their parents with the consequence that Quick-Fix Kids have a hard time taking criticism from teachers and principals, and later from boyfriends or bosses.

> *"I remember the look in my mom's eyes when she was giving me what you call a 'Quick-Fix' although I didn't know it at the time. What she was saying had nothing to do with me, she was just kind of glazed over with this fake smile. She would say how pretty I was, or how wonderful I was at this or that. Those are the exterior things that she saw and things that she could feel proud of herself about. Like my art, or swimming or whatever. I just never felt it was about me, and she didn't know how I really felt inside. I feel ungrateful because it doesn't sound that bad, that she would say those positive things. It is just that it never felt about me"*

Becoming dependent on quick-fixes, parents prevent the child from learning the life management skills that he needs to take care of himself, and from being concerned with others. Conduct disorders[3] result, in part, from a low concern for others. Those kids who are always getting in trouble, being taken into custody, spending time in

---

3 Conduct disorder" refers to a group of behavioral and emotional problems in youngsters. Children and adolescents with this disorder have great difficulty following rules and behaving in a socially acceptable way. They are often viewed by other children, adults and social agencies as "bad" or delinquent, rather than mentally ill. Many factors may contribute to a child developing conduct disorder, including brain damage, child abuse, genetic vulnerability, school failure, and traumatic life experiences. Go to http://www.aacap.org/cs/root/facts_for_families/conduct_disorder for more information.

hospitals or prisons, are those with low life-management skills. In a very non-satisfying way, they are being cared for by others.

Because they are used to getting what they want when they want it, kids develop low frustration tolerance. If kids are frustrated, parents think they're bad parents and carry on the cycle by using The Quick Fix, or whatever it will take to ease their kid's frustration and get rid of the irritation. Kids need to learn delayed gratification as kids (patience, self-control, will power, control of impulsive behavior and so on). If you are always or even sometimes Quick Fixing, you are robbing your kids of learning this.

"They must be happy. If they are happy, they will know that I love them."

#3 Cover for Abuse
In extreme cases, Quick Fixes can cover up abuse.

> *"My ex-husband would hit Jimmy again and again for the smallest mistake, and then when Jimmy was sobbing in his room, my ex would go in and ask if he'd like to go out with him to the sports store which he knew my son loved. I felt powerless to stop the hitting but in my screwed-up brain figured that at least he was taking him out after, so it wasn't that bad. Maybe secretly I let it all happen because I knew after the beatings that they would go out together and I really wanted them to spend more time together. And maybe I just wanted Jimmy out of the house. I didn't see how it was all connected and setting up a terrible pattern."*

Types of Quick-Fix Parents

#1 Don't Leave Type

Some parents want to keep their middle-aged children as children. They mourn every passage to adulthood; when toddlers are no longer toddlers, they mourn that they no longer have toddlers. When the last one goes to school, they mourn the babies who no longer need them. When teenagers leave home, they mourn the empty nest. Quick-Fix parents quiet their feelings of loss by keeping their children dependent and unwittingly buying into the entitlement they have created.

> *"I think all along I was mad at my kids for their entitlement and dependency, but I (and their father) created it. I don't think I wanted them to grow up and leave; I had never had the family I wanted, and I felt they hadn't either. I didn't want to let them go until we all got it right. So over the years I had bought into giving both children money—when I say bought in, the giving was often a result of manipulation. When my son-in-law asked me for a loan—I had offered to invest in his new company—I was torn. He told me he would repay me when his contract came through. On one hand I wanted to believe in him, but on the other hand I got an old familiar feeling. If I had the money, then they should have it especially if they needed it more than I did, and I would feel terrible if that money could get them to the point where they could be successful. I saw that guilt ran my actions then, and prevented me from seeing that they were just on a wrong path, and by adding money to it, I was*

making it worse. Since then they have both declared bankruptcy and the money is lost. The system they created took them to the condition they were in, and I was wrong to buy into it. I was saving that money for trips for myself and the grandkids, so I feel badly about it. But the mistake turned into a gift, because it detached me from the game once and for all, I hope."

#2 Giving-In to Every Whim Type

Giving is a great quality, but the Quick-Fix parent replaces parenting with quick-fixes ... too much stuff, and too little time. Some 'giving' parents believe they are helping their kids by giving them what they never had when they were children. They are trying to fix their own childhoods. They are quick-fixing themselves by quick-fixing their children. When parents quick-fix their children, they are not teaching their children to manage life. So, quick-fixed children become over-dependent on their parents, and do not gradually learn how to manage life. For this reason, quick-fixed children will often resent their parents. Instead of getting close to their children, they tend to separate from their parents except when they want another toy, money or a special activity.

"My daughter feels like she was deprived of candy as a child; that I withheld candy from her; while her father not only offered it, but used it as a special, secret gift. He would tell them not to tell me that he had given them candy. I don't know exactly where the abuse lies in all that, but my daughter resents me

*because she didn't get much candy from me,
whereas her dad indulged her."*

#3 Status-Driven Type

*"I remember how important houses and
home were to my mom. I can understand
why! She was sent away to a school at age
five where she lived until the end of high
school. She never had a home of her own,
and even as a young child, would admire
and envy the homes of the other girls in the
convent. Mom almost never left for any of
the holidays. No wonder homes were
important to her. It was a given that
wherever we lived, we were moving ahead
and working toward a better home. Mom
finally worked it so we bought our own
home when I was about 10 years old. It was
in a really good neighborhood, and Mom
wanted so much to fit in with those higher
than us on the socioeconomic scale, even
though we couldn't afford it.*

*I think my drive for a beautiful home
resulted from mom's drive. It was built into
me, and I saw family and closeness
intricately tied up with quality of home. I
was trying to meet my mother's needs, and I
know I passed that off to at least one of my
children."*

Some "giving" parents feel competition with other
parents, who are also quick-fixing their children. To keep
up, they "keep-up-with-the-Jones" in their lavish gifts and
constant clothes shopping.

"We lived across the street from the perfect couple with the perfect house and I got obsessed with being good enough, matching whatever they had or were doing. I don't know if it was just that, but we spent $75,000 that we didn't have on landscaping, money that should have gone into my children's education fund. I was always shopping for new clothes for the kids, and they always had the latest Bratz doll and all the clothing. We have spent so much money on all those things for the kids and just ended up giving them all away. In the end, the kids don't care, but I sure did."

#4 Fixing Parents' Mistakes Type

Quick-Fix parents believe their parents raised them wrong, and are determined to correct their own parents' mistakes, by becoming perfect parents.

"I will fix my childhood, by replaying my childhood through my children. I will be a child-centered parent and give my children everything they want, to make sure they are happy. I will be the perfect parent my parents never were. If I do this, I will be a good parent and my children will be happy." It comes as a bit of a shock, when these dedicated parents begin to notice that things are not going the way they had planned. They don't understand why their kids don't listen to them. They are perfect parents with perfect children. It truly is head-scratching for them.

When parents practice this creed, their sole purpose is to wipe out their own parents' mistakes. They will make

47

their children happy, by being better parents than the parents who raised them. Instead, these parents create a new set of mistakes. Because they raise their children based on parenting they wanted from their own parents, the real needs that their actual children have are obscured. They view their children through the blinders of their own childhood.

#5 Guilty Type

Ah, guilt, the gift that keeps on giving. Often divorced parents try to release their guilt through excessive giving.

by Mark Parisi

Cartoon printed with permission.

Kids of guilt-ridden Quick-Fix parents learn at a young age how to guide their parents toward guilt-reducing purchases. They are really talented at it.

> *"I don't know how we always ended up at Toys-R-Us. He would just have that sad look, or say something about how he wishes we were a family again. I see it now, that I would always take him to the toy store, like an automatic lever he would pull. I couldn't stand him looking sad and he was really good at it. I wished I had let him be sad and talked about the sadness, but I couldn't see it or stand it at the time."*

#6 If-You-Don't-Stop-Doing-That-This-Minute Type

This quick-fix variety appears to be encouraging their children toward appropriate behavior, but there are too many warnings, too little follow though. There will be threat after threat about what will happen when the kid does whatever it is one more time, but nothing ever happens! What a deal!

"If I've told you once, I've told you 1,000 times, don't bang your fork on the table."

"If you don't stop doing that, I will take away your privileges for a month."

"If you get home late one more time, you lose the car forever."

> *"So I remember I would get control in this weird game of make-dad-a-crazy-person, and I would always win, because there never*

> *was a follow through. If dad by chance did take away privileges (and he would always go way overboard because he was mad and not thinking), he would forget about it the next day and anyway, I was so good at manipulating him that he'd give in the second day."*

So it's a no-lose for the quick-fix kid; he gets away with a fun behavior (like kicking the wall), he gets front row center seat at his parents drama, and he gets a bonus afterwards when he kicks into his parent's guilt system and gets a bonus prize. It would be a great system if it wasn't destroying his character.

Some "if-I-told-you-once" parents think they are disciplining their children and providing guidance, but they fear taking action. Wanting to be friends with their children, and not lose their 'love', they fear that real discipline will hurt the relationship. Most lack assertiveness. Parenting isn't the only area where they lack influence; they struggle with spouses, supervisors, in-laws, landlords, and so on. They hope that others will simply respond to their warnings. Rarely do they take any actions to either advance their lives or discipline their kids.

What's Going on with Quick-Fix Parents:

1. Denial

When teenagers do exert their independence, which may or may not include parents' hopes and fantasies, some parents, stuck in denial, strive to keep their original fantasies alive. Parents deny reality as they preserve a fantasy that their children are perfect.

> *"I didn't know there was a problem, I really didn't. I mean I saw food chunks on the edge of the bathtub and couldn't figure out how it got there. After a while I wondered if anyone was throwing up, it looked like that. But how could that be? I'm not sure how I processed it. When my 19-year-old daughter admitted herself into the hospital for treatment of bulimia, I was in shock. How did that happen? What went wrong? I was really confused. It showed me how detached I was from what was going in with her, that I wasn't even tracking my daughter's life, much like my life had never been tracked by my parents. And when family day came around at the hospital, her father refused to have anything to do with it. He didn't want to deal with unpleasantness. It was his own daughter's life and he didn't want to deal with it. That's what she grew up with, a mother who wasn't really tracking and a father who didn't want to deal with it."*

Because they want to believe that they are good parents they decide also that, "My children are right and others are wrong." Parents will edit out information from reliable resources (teachers, friends, school counselors) that is inconsistent with their beliefs about their children.

In a sense, they almost see their children as victims; this is especially true if the parent's role in the world also is as a victim. With much unexpressed victim anger, angry parents will easily ally with their children when they are upset. This lets parents express their anger at targets outside the home. They unleash their anger at anyone who criticizes their children, even those who offer real concerns.

"If one of the children misbehaves, he or she must have a good reason." These parents believe they are protecting their children by blaming others for their children's behavior. If a teacher has a conflict with a child, parents will blame the teacher. They immediately believe their children, and blame any opposing party. They rarely consider their children's role. These parents will sometimes blame one teacher (coach, principal, friend) for destroying their children's lives such that their children, believing themselves blameless, learn to blame others instead of learning to manage conflict.

It's a clean setup. When parents blame others, they can avoid personal responsibility and the discomfort of facing themselves. If a family of five blames someone outside their family, five people are off the hook and avoid taking responsibility.

2. It's My Fault

Some parents cooperate by taking the blame themselves. Of course, when they blame themselves, they stop their children from taking responsibility. If *It's My Fault* parents believe they cause their children's problems, they see no reason to discipline them. So the children to continue to act out, without correction. There is safety in blaming themselves for their children's behavior. As long as they can attribute the problem to *it's-all-my-fault*, there is no need to look underneath and discover the real problem and fix it.

By rescuing their kids by taking the blame, they feel they are helping their kids, by giving them a sense of empowerment. Think about it. When a parent takes the blame for a child's behavior, the child will feel fixed (better) but never learns to correct his behavior.

3. Rose-Colored Glasses

Some parents just don't believe in discipline, either because underneath they hold the erroneous belief that if they were really good parents their kids wouldn't need discipline, or they believe discipline harms the natural development of children. These Quick-Fixers mean no harm. To create high self-esteem in their children, they believe their children should receive only positive messages.

Rose-Colored parents have a super quality of recognizing the good in people. They praise their kids, they find the good in others and the world, always looking on the bright side. Sadly, they are unable to recognize and evaluate the negatives. So the quick-fix kid grows up uncorrected and begins to believe that he doesn't have any flaws. He is heading toward a strong narcissistic attitude and the beginnings of a Narcissistic Personality Disorder[4].

Some Rose-Colored parents go a step further and tell their children they are gifted, when they really are not, forming a narcissistic layer of pride around the child. They exaggerate their children's positive characteristics or see incredible qualities within their children, which aren't there. Their children are the best of all. Many children believe that they will be the natural leaders of their class, but without the ability to form connections, to deeply

---

4 Narcissistic personality disorder is a disorder in which people have an inflated sense of their own importance and a deep need for admiration. They believe that they're superior to others and have little regard for other people's feelings. Behind this mask of ultra-confidence lies a fragile self-esteem, vulnerable to the slightest criticism. Narcissistic personality disorder is one of several types of personality disorders. Personality disorders are conditions in which people have traits that cause them to feel and behave in socially distressing ways, limiting their ability to function in relationships and in other areas of their life, such as work or school. In particular, narcissistic personality disorder is characterized by dramatic, emotional behavior, in the same category as histrionic, antisocial and borderline personality disorders.

recognize the needs of others, and to delay gratification, they often fail. When the world points out these problems in the child, these children become shocked. Instead of being able to correct themselves, they react with hostility, anger, withdrawal, and sometimes rage.

These parents believe that nature has offered them a perfect child. Sometimes they are competitive with other parents. To get an edge, they see only the good in their own children, and spot the bad in other children. Admitting their children have flaws is an admission of being a bad parent. Their self-esteem is wrapped around the image of their perfect children. If they accept their kids' problems, they are lowering their own self-esteem. To feel good about themselves, they have to see their children as perfect.

Usually these parents are not happy with their own lives, which can understandably lead them to want to hype up some part of their life. Children are handy targets. Sometimes there is one rose-colored parent that hypes the children, while the other parent has a more accurate picture. The rose-colored parent seems to everyone to be the better parent and is often favored by the kids. The more realistic parent seems too critical.

> *"My dad just was so accepting, no matter*
> *what. I felt so accepted by him and I miss*

that. I remember Mom and Dad having a conversation about our self-esteem, mom was worried that it wasn't higher. Dad told her she was full of nonsense, that it was fine. Mom saw what was going on and wanted help fixing it, but dad couldn't see any of it. He never wanted to talk about anything unpleasant. Looking back, Dad accepted things he shouldn't have I guess."

4. I Want to Be Friends

No description needed here. Be friendly, but you cannot be a buddy or a friend. Get those needs met elsewhere. You serve many purposes, but a friend is not one of them. Friends don't discipline friends, but parents discipline children. Friends are not legally responsible for their friends, but parents are legally responsible for their children.

5. Fear of Conflict

"Don't Be Mad at Me" A parent who sets limits risks conflict. Their fear of conflict is so strong, they often give their kids permission to do whatever they want, rather than confront their children with limits. The emotional backlash of arguments, pouting, and crying is just too much for their skill level.

6. "I Was the Favorite"

Some Quick-Fix parents will focus on one child only, not needing the fix from the others. There is a quality in the child that ties into the needs of the parent, and this quality

by Mark Parisi

Cartoon printed with permission.

is chosen by the quick-fix parent. Some kids are just good at sucking up and getting favored. Other children in the family feel neglected and are usually the angry and acting-out kids. As young children, they rarely become angry with the parent who offers the favoritism (it is just too dangerous; they might lose the attachment with this parent altogether). Instead, they get angry with the favored child, and often with the other parent.

> *"My sister was about five years older than I was, and I never really remember her much from childhood, except that we fought. She hated me and I never knew why. I bought into it, I would bug her and she would get mad at me, and mom would come in and get mad at her. I was the favored one anyway, and knew how to act to get mom's sympathy. It always worked. Later on she would say things to me like I caused my dad's mental illness, and that I should be in the psych hospital. I didn't realize that she was acting normally for a disfavored child. It wasn't until 60 years later that we began to see how it all played out. I am not sure that she sees*

> *that being favored was just as damaging as being non-favored, but at least I know it."*
>
> *"My sister is just under two years younger than I am, and she was favored by my dad and probably mom after a while too. She was all sweet and complimentary even as a young kid and my dad ate it up. She also was sick when she was little, and my dad had been sick as child so I think he identified with that too. My mom was never sick and didn't have much tolerance for weakness or being sick. I started acting up and getting mad, and nobody knew what to do about it. My dad didn't know how to handle anger, so I was mad at mom primarily. Mom and Dad divorced and he moved out, and he often just wanted my sister to visit. And I beat up my sister whenever I could. I am just getting over the belief that there is something wrong with me because I have been so angry all my life."*

Some quick-fix parents, who favor one child, over-identify with the child they prefer. A shy parent may over-identify with a shy child, or over-identify with the warm, social child. This over-identification promotes a quick attachment between parent and child that doesn't happen with the other children. In a similar vein, a parent may have a favorite skill and the child who excels in this skill, becomes the favored child. Whatever, these parents naturally favor one child above the rest. Other parents, who play favorites, recognize that one of their children is vulnerable. They assume that their other children don't need special attention (but they do).

Needy parents train children to learn how to respond to their parents' neediness and get favored attention. Children always learn by trial and error, how to get their parents' attention. The children who are better at reading their parents' needs, become favored children. The other children, who do not read their parents' needs, receive less attention.

7. Exploding

This style really confuses kids. Typically nonassertive, skill-deficient parents unpredictably explode with anger and rant at their children and then, take it all back and blame themselves. The layers of tension in these families are thick, and these families avoid discussing any family issues that might ignite emotions. Convenient!

Dig underneath the surface and find simmering rage, ready to blow. Why so much rage? With such a high degree of passivity, these folks never learned to stand up for themselves. Lacking assertiveness, they allow others to mistreat them creating a brewing anger. These parents can be legitimately angry with their children, as well, but instead of learning how to express their upset feelings, they withhold their hurts and allow them to brew.

By not asserting themselves, they get frustrated, and like a pipe that is gradually wearing thinner and thinner, at unpredictable times they explode at the safest targets (the kids). Since they often are intelligent, introspective people, they realize after the blow up that the kids are not the real source of their anger, so they make up for it and quick-fix their children.

8. Be Happy

"I want my kids to be happy." "I want to protect my child from ever feeling uncomfortable emotions." These parents believe that by giving kids a steady stream of fun and happy experiences, and avoiding painful emotions, they will create high self-esteem kids. They will do almost anything to prevent their children from having painful emotions. They believe that being a good parent equals the number of happy experiences parents can provide for their children. With this definition of happiness, many parents push a constant stream of happy experiences onto their children, only to be disappointed with the outcome.

> *"I am exhausted, just exhausted. I have three boys aged four, two, and one just two months old. My eldest son's fourth birthday was last week. I themed a Spiderman party with Spiderman invitations (with my son's face inserted onto the Spiderman body), hired Spiderman to entertain, had a Spiderman jumping thing, Spiderman food and gift bags, Spiderman whatever else. About two dozen adults were there and maybe 15 little kids. The gifts were piled deep under the Spiderman table. I took photos with my new Canon 4D and posted them and sent out themed thank you notes to everyone. I feel I should be doing more, I*

just want them to be happy, I don't know why
I am so tired all the time."

Buying happiness is easy! In the North American culture, buying happy items like toys and fun activities is easy. Drive through any McDonald's and buy a "Happy Meal." Go to happy Chuckie Cheese! With excessive giving, parents convince themselves their children are happy. If they only quick-fix their children, their children are not learning to manage life.

9. "I Want it My Way!"

A lingering theme in our culture is the old Burger King slogan, 'Have it your Way'. We want fulfillment in every part of lives, including career, money, advancement, high-end cars, exiting marriages, and having kids. Sadly, having it all is not possible, or desirable, certainly not with the time and money constraints of parents with young children. With the 'I Want it My Way!' parents, children seem to exist to fill the needs of parents. Parents think they can work their children into their busy lifestyles. So they send their children to a happy day care, buy them happy toys, send them to happy activities, but they are 'off the deal' when it comes to spending quality time and being really involved with their kids. Quick-Fix parents convince themselves their children are happy, because they have so many happy things. Parents continue to have it their way, until their children become teenagers, detach from parents, and develop problems that do demand and get parental attention.

Many 'I want' parents say that they both need to work to have a good home, so they can raise happy children. They send their children away from their home to a daycare, and never see the irony.

> *"I went to school full time, worked part-time, and raised my two daughters alone. My story was that with an advanced degree I could get a better job, we could move to a better home, I would meet a better partner and we would all be happier. Along the way I didn't notice that they were being dragged through my life, with the focus on what I needed and wanted. I even moved them across the continent to a new country. Ironically, they returned to our hometown last month for the funeral of their father, and went back to visit the small upper duplex where they were raised. I was always embarrassed by it, but I know where that comes from now. What got me is that they both said what warm and happy memories they had of the duplex, and the small park across the street. How little all the other stuff meant–the degree, the money, the whatever. I wish I knew then what I know now, but I have to keep focusing on no-regrets"*

10. No-Maybe-Yes

Quick-Fix parents have a hard time with decisions. When their kids sulk and whine, it's an invitation to begin to negotiate. They want their children to feel as though they are part of the decision-making process. When parents negotiate, their goal is to be fair to both parties; nagging kids don't care, they just want to win.

Filled with ambivalence and confusion, Quick-Fix parents teach their children that not every parental decision is a final one; all decisions are negotiable. Most ambivalent parents don't like making decisions at all. Needing to avoid the responsibility that comes with making decisions, they shift decision-making to other employees, to friends, to the waitress, to their spouse and to their kids.

When parents think children should have equal status with adults in their family, with good intentions they give children too much decision-making power, believing they are building children's self-esteem. In reality, when children make decisions before they are capable, they are setup to fail, harming them in the end.

If you recognized yourself in any of those descriptions, it's only good news. The descriptions seem negative, but create awareness. You can't change it unless you see it.

Chapter Three
Who are Quick-Fix Kids?

They are neat kids, sometimes talented, often attractive, and certainly tuned in to their parents (or supervisor's) soft spots. They are charming until they don't get what they want. They have learned to develop much manipulative talent, and charm is part of their cycle. When Quick-Fix Kids get too much power, they don't have the thinking capacity to manage it, they just feel pressure to take charge of their families. Instead of creating healthy families, they need to try to prove they are the most powerful person in their pack.

Quick-Fix children are so busy with pack leadership, they never learn their limits or learn how to manage life.

We've already sorted out that children need clear guidelines. With parents who do not make firm decisions, children are always trying to discover their limits. When everything is negotiable, there are no limits. These

65

children constantly question how far they can go– it's just natural.

When children make decisions they are too young to make, they are taking on a life for which they are not prepared. Their decisions are guaranteed to be bad ones. Forced into adult decisions, their fragile egos either become inflated, or they become excessively dependent. As adults, they feel that life's decisions are filled with too much pressure. Instead of seeing decision-making as a tool to manage life, they see it as a dreaded responsibility to avoid. They would rather be dependent on others and lose the ability to make good decisions.

1. Dependent

Quick-Fix creates dependencies. Dependencies create anger and resentment. Children whose parents quick-fix, often become dependent because their parents are not teaching them to be independent.

Parents expect love for the gifts they offer, but instead, they get an angry and resistant child who doesn't respect or listen.

Kids who don't receive consequences for bad behavior, are failing to gain skills they will need for adult social, financial, emotional health. Psychologically healthy adults have gradually learned skills to manage life and its complications through childhood, adolescence, and adulthood. Quick-fixed children who have not "learned to listen" are not learning the skills to manage life.

When we quick-fix, we deny our kids the chance to recognize that a problem exists, to consider their contribution to the problem, and to fix the problem and make amends to anyone they have hurt.

1. Dependency
2. A lack of skills
3. An inflated ego.

This is psychic turmoil for children. On the one hand, quick-fix parents inflate their children's ego by aggrandizing positive qualities, but on the other hand, not giving them life management skills.

2. Persistent

Quick-Fix Kids are persistent. Once rewarded, they can and will use the same strategy forever and ever. This is a valuable trait when it is turned in another direction, and focused on achievement.

3. Entitled

When people get something for nothing, people want more for nothing. When parents give everything kids want, kids want more! Parents really do believe that through excessive giving, they will prove their love and they hope that their children will respond with love. Instead, the kids want more! How can these quick-fixed children gain love attachments? Having grown up with resentment and entitlement, it is all they know in relationships. I want more!

If kids don't learn self-reliance, and only have dependency, they develop real skill at demanding more. Others should provide for them, and it would be very self-centered of the parents not to provide for their every whim. There is a mixture of dependency and arrogance in the expectation that others provide for them.

For example, Dad buys himself a $60k Mercedes, his kid wants it, and in defiance he keys dad's car. Dad says, "Screw it, then, I'll buy you the car." So he gets a matching Mercedes for the kid. An 8-year-old wasn't showing up at school. During a home visit, the school psychologist heard the child ask if he could sit on a certain chair. Mom is sitting in the chair and gets up.

"She looked at me–stared, really–and told me that other parents gave their children money for mortgages. She had asked me for about $20,000. I felt torn; I had enough money to live on and was saving for retirement. I wanted to help, and wanted to see myself as a loving helpful parent and I guess I wanted her and everyone else to think of me that way too. That was the real problem looking back. And guilt for a number of things I suppose. So I gave her the money. There wasn't a lot of gratitude, and I noticed that her charming self gradually dissipated when she got what she wanted and wasn't after something."

"My daughter (married with three children in her mid-30's) was graduating from college with her Master's degree. Of course, we were all proud of her. She decided that she wanted a party and that I (her mother) should pay for it. She was her best charming self as she outlined the hotel, the rooms the guests would need, the food, the party itself. I felt like I was in my worst nightmare right then, and couldn't believe that she was really asking me this. I mean, I never had a party like this, people don't throw big parties for these things. They certainly didn't have the money to do it, and neither did I. When I told her I couldn't throw the party, but could help with a part of it, she blew up and starting yelling at me about how snobbish I was that I had graduated from a better university than she had, and that I was dismissing her accomplishment because her university was second rate. After that, there has been a coldness between us that I don't think has gone away. It's too bad–I know her father and I caused this originally, but I am not the one to fix it for her."

69

4. Relationship Problems

Quick-Fix Kids never learn the give-and-take of relationships. Although they are good at engaging with others, it is only to get others to meet their needs. They tend to not be able to make emotional connections ... no wonder, since the parents are not consistently engaged.

5. Resentful

Quick-fixed kids become naturally resentful of their parents about their dependency, but they have no skills to achieve independence. Over-dependency and resentment grow, until there is a breakdown in the parent-child relationship. These children become emotionally distant with their parents as adults. Why?

When a child behaves inappropriately and a responsible parent disciplines and guides the child, the parent has made the child 'attach'. For example, a nine-year-old boy carved his name on the wooden railing of his school. The school disciplined him, but his father and the child went to school the next day to fix the railing. He watched as his son sandpapered the railing, and he taught his son to stain and varnish. For the next two days, he returned to school, so his son could apply two more coats of varnish.

This father disciplined, but also allowed his son to attach. This father required that his son make a physical and emotional attachment to the school too, by fixing the railing. Quick-Fix parents do not require their children to do this type of attachment, so they become emotionally distant.

> *"We always blamed Mother Johnson. My father would write her letters complaining about her discipline at Sacred Heart. We always played innocent, that we were being mistreated by her at the school. She was over-the-top with her discipline, and favored some kids over others, but deep down we knew we did things wrong."*

Discipline does need to teach and guide children on how to behave, but children should also feel the emotional component of discipline. Does the child's behavior create disappointment? Sadness? Anger?

For example, your child Mary's friend Jeanne says she is going to come over to play with her, but often does not show up. She invites Jeanne to go to a show, but then goes with someone else, leaving Mary at home. Every time she lets her down, Mary feels the emotional pain of disappointment, teaching a valuable lesson, "Don't count on Mary." If Mary thought about it, she would decide to find a better friend.

If Mary did not feel this emotional pain, she would never end the relationship and learn from her previous experiences. The same is true when children feel painful emotions about themselves; they are able to create change in themselves. If Quick-Fix parents prevent or rescue this emotional pain, they fail to develop the skill to create self-change. They stop their children from learning lessons about themselves.

Chapter Four
Changing the System

Your quick-fixed children won't tell you that they need love, bonding, discipline, and limits, but they do. They will be mad at you when you start to set limits, but saying no at the right time is the most important skill a parent can develop.

When you make changes, the changes you undergo can be threatening and thus intolerable to other people in your life. Let's use an 'adult' example. In 'codependent' relationships, where boundaries cross like two concentric circles, one partner's denial can depend upon the other partner's symptoms. For example, Shawna and Jim had developed an 'unconscious' agreement, meaning that they were not aware of the secret agreement they had. Although both really wanted a

73

healthy relationship, the past, unrecognized patterns were stronger than new awareness or behavior.

This was the typical downward spiral: Jim would forget an agreement, Shawna would react with anger and continue the anger as sarcasm for several hours. After an hour or two, Jim would react negatively to her sarcasm and with righteous indignation, stomp out of the house and head for the bar. He tells himself that he doesn't deserve this treatment, and anybody in his situation would do the same thing. This would confirm Shawna's unconscious belief that all men are weak and Jim's belief that all women are nags, confirm their own inability to be loved, and the futile nature of relationships. Phew.

This reasoning prevented them from confronting the real nature of the addictions they both had, prevented them from developing intimacy, and kept the precarious balance alive. As long as Jim would forget something, Shawna would have that or a similar reaction, and off they would go, Jim's alcoholism justified.

Now, what would happen to this balance if Jim stopped drinking? What would happen if Shawna decided not to use sarcasm as a weapon? The game would be up, or at least, the balance would be lost. How could Jim then justify his drinking? How could Shawna support her belief that all men are weak? Something would have to change! Sounds like a soap opera, doesn't it!

It takes both partners to maintain the balance, and if one

changes, the other must. If the changes are made consciously, both partners can work through the balance and develop new, healthier responses. Changes can create such an imbalance in the relationship that the partner who is not changing works to keep things the same, or develops symptoms himself.

If an alcoholic stops drinking, the nagging spouse either needs to find another outlet, or stop nagging and using him as an excuse. If an overweight partner loses weight, the partner needs to confront the new personality that emerges and face the threat of the loss of the fat cushion around his partner. His partner is suddenly more attractive to the opposite sex, and this could be a threat that he is not up to. Parents whose focus is on an aberrant child often work unconsciously to keep the child a problem, even though they would certainly deny this. If the child were to improve, they would need to focus on and face their own relationship, which they cannot do.

These balances exist to some degree in all relationships, but that doesn't mean that they're all unhealthy, and it doesn't mean that changes can't be made. Be on guard for sabotage from folks around you who might, or might not, be 'needing' your symptoms to justify their own dysfunction.

Thus, sometimes we might find that the 'reward' for our effort to grow and change is that our loved ones fight us at every step of the way, or even leave us. If this happens, we need to gather people around us who support our growth, cut the rope on the others, and free them up to live at the level they wish.

**When you start to change your system,
one that worked very well for everyone else,
expect some desperate attempts to resist.**

For many years, children have come to expect certain behaviors, emotions, consequences or lack of them, and changes will be upsetting.

Get out of the cycle:
It is not useful to dig around the past looking for answers to current problems. That doesn't mean you shouldn't visit the past to find out decisions you made then, and to question whether these decisions that you made based on

your environment then, are the right decisions for you now (chances are they weren't).

So know the impact of the past, but know it happened in the past. You did the best you could. They did the best they could. Resentment, revenge, depression, guilt, and other forms of angst just aren't going to change it. You prevent yourself from changing by deciding to hang on to the pain. As long as you are digging around the past, your flashlight can't be focused on the future.

Let it go. Let it go.

Letting it go doesn't mean that what they did was right or good, nor what you did was right or good, or the best example of parenting there was. It was the best that there was at the time, and if you had known better and if they had known better, everybody would have done better. Those are sentences to repeat several times a day until you get it. Decide to have no regrets about the past.

The point is: what are you going to do about it now? As my friend Gil Eagles, a talented east-coast hypnotist and stage performer says, "Guess what? Now what?" Guess what? It happened. Go right to: "Now what are you going to do about it?" without stopping in the middle.

Some parents who were abused, continue the cycle of abuse with their own children, it just looks different. Other parents stop the generational abuse cycle. Most of those who stop the abuse cycle review past abuses, with a special intent. If they gain a sensitive understanding of the effects of abuse in their lives, they also understand the effects on their children. This sensitive insight stops them from hurting their children. So, they review their past to gain insights to effectively change their current lives, with the hope of a better future without abuse. Go visit, but don't live there.

Do not waste your life 'scapegoating' your parents. When your children model their angry parents, it is easy for them to start scapegoating their parents (which is you). Work it out.

What to Do

Get immune to sulking, nagging, and whining. They are not real emotions, but manipulative games. Be calm. Do not respond. You can pull a Rumpelstiltskin[5] if the child is old enough (over five or six years old). "I see you are sulking, pretending to be sad. Although you are doing a good job at sulking, you are not doing a good job at persuading me to give in to you. That won't work. If you want something, it is best to just ask for it. Then either you get it or not, but at least we don't go through all this drama."

"If you want the train set, I can show you how to earn enough money to buy it, but I am not giving it to you."

Children need to learn to earn what they get. When you teach your children to work, you're also teaching them to save money, be responsible, plan, carry out the stuff of life. It's all good.

---

5 Rumpelstiltskin is a character in a Grimm's Brothers Fairy Tale. To make himself appear more important, a miller lied to the King that his daughter could spin straw into gold. The King called for the girl, shut her in a tower room with straw and a spinning wheel, and demanded that she spin the straw into gold by morning, for three nights, or be executed. She had given up all hope, when a dwarf appeared in the room and spun straw into gold for her in return for her necklace; then again the following night for her ring. On the third night, when she had nothing with which to reward him, the strange creature spun straw into gold for a promise that the girl's first-born child would become his. The King was so impressed that he let the miller's daughter marry his son, the Prince, but when their first child was born, the dwarf returned to claim his payment: "Now give me what you promised". The Queen was frightened and offered him all the wealth she had if she could keep the child. The dwarf refused but finally agreed to give up his claim to the child if the Queen could guess his name in three days. At first she failed, but before the second night, her messenger overheard the dwarf hopping about his fire and singing. When the dwarf came to the Queen on the third day and she revealed his name, Rumpelstiltskin lost his bargain, and he ran away angrily, and never came back.

There are no substitutes or excuses for truth and honesty. Give kids advance consequences for lying. Lying is an attempt at attention; ask yourself if you're giving enough attention without lying.

Tell your kids "When you try to manipulate me with guilt, you are insulting me."

Negotiation never works with nagging, whining, and children.

Note: Quick-Fix parents are excessively trusting. They're gullible. Children can learn to be amazingly talented actors. A sulking kid's sadness is acted, but so well that it works. When parents buy into the act, control shifts to the child. You need to stop buying in!

Here are the basics first:
*Think carefully about what rules or behaviors are important, those you won't budge on.
*Get everyone in the house on the same page about these.

*Get clear and consistent with your child about these. Kids cannot read your mind. They shouldn't 'just know' what to do.

*Don't enforce rules when you're too angry or drained to think straight and get it right. In those times, give a Calm Delay[6] and wait until you get it together, then approach.

*Never yell or hit. These are out of control behaviors putting your child back in power. If you happen to forget that, just apologize, and get back on track.

*Reward your child only when he or she is following the rules, and in a calm state. Think out the rewards ahead of time, consulting with your child.

When you are ready:
Reestablish Communication

Talk to your child. Say, "We have gotten way off track, and it has been my fault. I take responsibility, and I am sorry. We need to get back on track, to make this family work better, and to set up a better way. Together we will do that."

Your tone of voice is calm, but in charge. Your sentence tone drops at the end, instead of rises. Commands are firm, short, and to the point.

---

6 "Right now, I need some time to pull it together and to think a bit straighter. So I'm going on a time-out for about 10 minutes, and in 10 minutes we'll meet here in the living room"

Redo Basic Training

To start this system in early childhood–teach your child your language–combine words with an action that shows the child what you want, and some reinforcement, either positive or negative. Say your child's name. Your child should have a pleasant experience when s/he hears his name–not unpleasant. Some people create a new 'Punishment' name to use for those times. To teach the child his name, position your child close enough to touch. Say the name cheerfully and gently move his face in your direction. When the child looks in your direction, immediately use your reinforcing voice. Practice this until looking at you happens without your assistance and continue to practice for the child's entire life! It reinforces the communication link between the parent and child. By the way, if this sounds as though it is out of a dog manual it is. Told you. I think it is brilliant.

Teach other words the same way. Simple commands work best. Say the child's name (to get his attention), follow with a command, and then show him what you want. Praise immediately when the action is completed. Eventually your child will learn to respond to the command without needing to be shown, but don't forget to praise. "Susan, turn off the television. Good job, that's the way." "Susan, come here and sit down. Good work".

Clarify the New Order

Sometimes words are not enough when communicating with a child. Since children must learn what each word means, all the other "extra" words are just a bunch of "blah, blah". A modified 'kidspeak' can get a child's attention faster than human words. The word "no" to a child is a comfortable, soft word, with no sharp sound to it. Therefore there is nothing in the word to catch a child's attention, or to stop them from continuing the action you wish to halt. A rough, gravelly 'EGH!' can be used to stop them from doing things. This dog stuff is good.

Establish Pack Values

Every pack has fundamental values upon which their survival is based. Safety and honesty are basic pack values. "It is agreed that in this pack we will keep you safe and you will learn to trust us." Without safety and honesty, the basic building blocks of character never get constructed.

Pack Leader parents appreciate people's differences in culture and background. They see all people as equal. They teach their children to be accepting of others. They also love their children equally and teach their children to take care of others, inside and outside their families. However, they realize that equally loving their children does not mean that they raise their children the same. Children are unique and, although they can offer equal love, they reserve the right to raise children according to their unique differences.

What are your values? Choose a few central values, such as honesty, and make sure they show up everywhere, and you make decisions around them.

If I had have known better, I would have done better.

Chapter Five:
Ground Rules

Here are non-negotiable changes you must make if you want others to listen to you.

1. Spend time hanging
out with your kids.

If you drag them through your life, that's not quality time. You can't positively influence your children if you don't want to spend time with them. We are good at spending time with our babies and toddlers, but somewhere along the line we go astray, and discover other priorities. We are relieved when our kids are at camp or when grandma takes them for a day or two. When they are home we like when they are engrossed in their TV programs or hobbies. Why is that? What happened?

Kids have daily emotional needs that need immediate attention that can't be fixed by a purchase so that you can have more time to pursue other avenues of your life. Engage with your kids on all issues. Tell the truth about everything, even those things you are embarrassed about. Who is that man, mom? Why were you out late last night, mom? Are you making fudge, dad? Did you have plastic surgery, mom? How did grandpa die, dad? What is the letter from the tax collector about, dad?

2. Tell the truth, no matter what.

Truth will really set you free; you will get over the embarrassment. So your kids put the item in the *Daily Tribune*. Tomorrow it will be yesterday's news, but your relationship will be stronger and will live forever.

Lie to your kids today, you'll be spared the news story, but you'll also lose the relationship with your children. Is it worth it? Have a deep commitment to truth and reality–especially truth and reality that is painful.

> *"I remember asking my mom about the can of shaving cream in the bathroom. She said she used it to shave her legs, and I knew she was lying. It turned out that her boyfriend put it there, but I guess she was trying to spare us the truth or was confused about it*

herself. Anyway the net effect was that I didn't trust my mom to tell me the truth."

Truth is the foundation of a family. Without truth, families crumble. Have a deep commitment to truth, even in little matters. Show your kids at the grocery store that you don't accept change that doesn't belong to you. That you don't

by Mark Parisi

MOMMY, TELL ME THE TRUTH... IS IT REALLY YOU THAT LEAVES THE MONEY UNDER MY PILLOW?

©2003 MARK PARISI, DIST. BY UFS, INC   offthemark.com

THE TOOTHFAIRY'S DAUGHTER

Cartoon printed with permission

open packages, help yourself to snacks, and don't pay for them. Show your kids that you tell the truth to your friends when they ask you what you did this weekend, or on the phone if you are busy. Don't ever ask your children to lie for you. Children need to be able to rely on their parents to always tell them the truth. Children need the truth; lies create distortions in kids that never get fixed.

***When you tell the truth,
your child not only learns about reality
and how to deal with it, but learns to trust you.***

> *"My dad committed suicide by shooting himself, but my children were only five, three and almost one. What was I supposed to tell them? What would they have understood? I told them he was sick and had a heart attack, I figured they might understand that. I never thought of correcting it, I figured it would just go away. Later on they learned the truth, and I really don't know the impact it had on them. I really don't know."*

You want your kids to learn that if they want the straight goods about big emotional issues, to go to a parent because a parent won't lie to you.

Regarding explanations about traumatic scenes, it is true that younger children don't develop as many behavioral problems, aggression and fears as those after the age of seven or eight; younger children may be protected by their inability to fully understand any traumatic scenes they witness; teens are often more affected by their *parents'* reactions than are primary school age siblings.

Young children of five to seven years have a built-in buffer when facing family trauma. They haven't been around very long, and the first couple years of their life were vague, so they have less to grieve. Since they don't abstract, they can't see the full impact of what the loss or trauma means. So the truth won't affect them as much as you think. Truth is a great foundation when families face it together. Hiding and secrecy crack the very foundation of a family.

Children need to hear the truth about their positive behavior and their negative behavior. Give your kids honest feedback about their skills and their limits. Never exaggerate your children's strengths, or ignore their limits.

> *"When I was in grade three, I drew a picture of a crowd of people. I guess my teacher showed it to my mother, and made a comment. My mother went on and on about this picture as if it were a Van Gogh, it was puzzling. She told me that it was very detailed and showed I was very intelligent and showed a great deal of promise. Somehow this picture incident stands out in my memory, because usually my mother didn't pay much attention to me or my drawings. I don't know what effect that had, but I know that I felt pressured to be a great artist. I don't think I had any talent, beyond a sense of balance, and I don't think my mother ever noticed my work again. But I remember copying artist's works so I would win art prizes. I copied works on big canvases and hung them in the living room. I applied to the Ecole de Beaux Arts in Paris (and wasn't admitted). I bought books and books on art. I went to art galleries. I bought empty canvases and easels and paints that sat there doing nothing. Only last month I threw them out. I don't need to be an artist. Mom meant well, but I always felt that I let her down."*

Quick-Fix parents keep secrets to protect their children, instead of helping their children to manage the issues. When children realize their parents have a secret, distrust begins. Children wonder what other secrets exist. When parents talk to them about other important issues, children wonder if they are hearing the truth.

> *"I remember mom talking to Auntie Belle on the phone about my dad. She said he was in the hospital, but then she told us that he was on business. I could hear her because when I put my ear on my wall, the sounds from the kitchen were amplified. I could hear her clearly. I never asked her about that. I guess deep down I knew she couldn't take it. She was also scared to death about money. One day after she was talking to Auntie Belle and said how scared she was, I went into her bedroom. She was sitting on the edge of her bed with her books, crying. I asked her what was wrong. I didn't want to say that I had heard anything, I didn't know what to say. I wanted her to connect with me. She just said everything was all right. I mean she was crying, I knew what was wrong, and she lied to me. I think I gave up trying to connect with her."*

No secrets. You will have to learn to discuss sensitive issues because your job is to teach your children to manage sensitive issues. Secrets are lies. People who lie get inconsistent. Tell the truth so you can be consistent. Do you believe that a lie will protect your kids from emotional pain?

Children are 'truth detectors' who absorb every conversation and overhear every phone call. They notice subtle changes in their parents when they lie, and when certain topics come up. There will be people who inadvertently fill them in on the rest of the story. A boy's parent helped him look for his dog, who was

by Mark Parisi

I FOUND A MATCH AT THE STORE ON FIFTH AND MAIN. IT SHOULD BE CLOSE ENOUGH TO FOOL YOUR DAUGHTER...

PET STORE

GOLDFISH DATABASE

offthemark.com

Cartoon printed with permission

missing. The boy eventually heard from a friend that his dog was dead and the boy also learned that his parents knew the dog was dead; he was run over by a truck on the next street. His parents did not know that he learned the truth about his dog, and he never said anything. A little girl's bunny looked different one morning. She knew it was not her bunny, but her dad insisted it was. She found out from her sister that her bunny had died the evening before, and her dad had gone out a replaced the bunny. She never told her dad that she knew he was lying.

Kids hear secrets,
and they feel lies.

When we lie to protect our kids from emotional pain that is a natural part of life, although we mean well, we teach our kids that we are unsafe places to go when they feel pain, when they're upset. They never really learn how to manage the painful parts of life. When they become teenagers, and emotional issues become more complicated, we will lose their chance to have real influence because we have never formed a real attachment. Truth attaches, lies separate and isolate.

3. Don't do anything for them that they can do for themselves.

You can help your kids study for a test, but at some point, they have to take the test themselves. You can coach your teen on how to handle conflict with the school bully, but at some point he needs to manage the conflict on his own. Advise your kids with ideas to manage life, so they have what they need to do it start to manage life.

Quick-Fix parents take the reins from their children. They do it for their children. They do not give their children the skills to manage life.

"Ok I really didn't do her homework, but it happened too often that the time would fly by, and it was bedtime, and there was just a bit more to do. She would always say how desperate it was that she get it done and hand it in on time. I didn't want her to lose sleep, so I would finish it off for her, that's all. Oh I remember a time she had a giant project to do and the day before, when she came home for lunch, she was in panic because she didn't know it was due and it was a huge part of her final grade (she said). I felt so badly for her, and I had the time that day, so I did the research for her and kind of put it together. She did the handwriting under the pictures. I realize now how much rescuing I was doing; she was really good at getting me to believe that she didn't know about due dates and so on, and I was feeling guilty about the divorce and my schoolwork so I felt in a twisted way that I was making up."

4. Figure out your own identity, goals and dreams.

It's the parent's job to develop an identity before having children. When parents know themselves, their strengths and limits, and they are honest about them, they probably won't distort their children's talents. From the parent's own lack of understanding about their own identity comes the distorted labels harmful to children.

We'll talk more abut this in a later chapter, but what are your unmet goals and dreams? Any idea? Don't hang your unmet goals and dreams on your kids. If you do, your kids will feel pressure to meet your goals and dreams. When kids aim for their parents' unmet goals and dreams, they lose the opportunity to acquire their own dreams.

This is tough to figure out. Pack leader parents never give up on their own goals and dreams. So, instead of pressuring children to meet your unmet goals and dreams in life, create a list of your own goals and dreams and make them happen. If you are not actively working on your own path, chances are you may be putting too much pressure on your kids.

> "My mother finished high school, but always wanted to be more educated. Proper speech was very important to her, and developing manners of the educated and wealthy were close to the top. She did go back to night school for English courses, but I felt that she was so unhappy with her lot in life. We didn't have much money, she felt trapped at home with us, and she even needed to get a job when it wasn't cool for women to work. She told us she was staying with dad because of us. My sister and I have always been driven to improve ourselves, and obtain education that was probably beyond our level. In a way that was good, but the drive took precedence over more important things. My sister spent major time away from her family to go to school, and although I was at home I was preoccupied with my education so I might as well have been away. It was my mother's dreams we were fulfilling."

Watching parents strive toward their goals and dreams is great modeling for kids, but when their parents are living the dreams of someone else, there is no modeling is possible because attachment isn't possible. In the same vein, quick-fix parents can't distinguish their own unmet needs and wants, from those of their kids. So, they try to make their children happy by giving them what they wanted when they were children. Obviously this results in parents giving their kids what they neither want nor need, and parents end up frustrated too because it just doesn't work.

> "I always felt awkward at our family gatherings, after we grew up and had our own families. Mom was trying so hard to get us together and have a good time. There were even agendas for some of our family gatherings, like at Easter and Christmas. Things needed to happen in a certain way and at a certain time; we all felt like we were actors in my mom's play, something that she was trying to create for some unknown reason. She did put a lot of work into them, and at a level we appreciated it. But I don't think there was any real closeness, we didn't really feel attached. We all drank a fair amount then, so I guess that helped. Come to think of it, my mom stopped drinking alcohol about five years ago and we haven't had many gatherings since then. Maybe the wine helped us all get through it, and without it we don't know how to do family. I think that Mom never felt family closeness and was trying to meet her own deep needs through us, or maybe trying to create a family that she never had created for us when we were kids. "

Because Quick-fix parents want or need their children to stay dependent and at several levels, they prevent their children from self-reliance. They stop their children from taking the risks they need to become self-reliant by buffering either the exposure to opportunities or caution warnings.

> *"I think dad meant well; he was maybe genuinely concerned that something would happen to me. I was 18 years old, had finished high school, and I wanted to live in France for a year. I loved studying French, I wanted to take art classes, and I had saved up enough money to at least get over there. He never told me not to go, but he kept hinting at things that could happen. It was really subtle. I started wavering, but what really did it was that he started having chest pains about three months before I was going to leave. I just gave up and cancelled my plans to go, and I never did go. I went into nursing school instead. I try to live a no-regret life, but I often wonder what my life would have been had I had the strength to just go."*

5. Sort out
Love and Permissiveness

Unconditional love doesn't mean giving your kids everything they want. Unconditional love means letting children experience their own consequences for their misbehavior.

Unconditional love means accepting whatever
is happening with your child, accepting that he or
she needs to experience it, and
trusting that with your guidance, he or
she can navigate the way through.

Pack leader parents see clearly the results of their children's bad decisions, but let them experience the full range of consequences.

Quick-Fix parents confuse unconditional love with permissiveness, and have a strong need to buffer their children from the consequences of their behavior. With the belief "If my child has a negative emotional experience, it will hurt my child's self-esteem," Quick-Fix parents see discipline as hurting their child. There are fine lines between confidence, arrogance and sociopathy; applying the same rules to your child as society would apply creates confidence and responsibility. Letting your kid off the hook because he is special, or different, or

97

because someone else is always to blame, creates arrogance. Sociopathy results from a lack of attachment plus an exaggeration of a kid's special talents or abilities.

> *"My daughter refused to go to school unless she wore clothes from The Gap. I liked that she was trying to fit in, and that she felt so good about herself and such a great sense of style. It got really expensive after a while but when I tried to reduce the amount of the purchases or cut down on some of the items, I felt really guilty for some reason. I mean here she is, a vulnerable teen just trying to look good. I remember when I was a teen I always felt awkward and out of place and my mom made me wear my sister's old clothes. I hated it and I didn't want to put her through it."*

The difference between kid's 'needs' and 'wants' is easy to distinguish when you know how, hard when you are caught in the web of manipulation.

Wants and Needs

Quick-Fix parents have a hard time distinguishing between children's 'wants' and 'needs', often substituting 'wants' for 'needs' (it is easier, and requires less introspection). Quick-Fix parents give-in to all their children's requests, which results in quick-fix children being out of control. Many parents pay 24% interest on credit cards to get whatever their children want. They think they are giving unconditional love, when they are really training their children to feel entitled. When some parents quick-fix their children, they believe they are proving to themselves and others that they are good parents. They feel they have proved their value, because their children have many goodies and many freedoms.

Why can't some Quick-Fix parents say, "No"? When they say "Yes" they feel a comfort that convinces them that they are good parents. They are at their best when their children are smiling, after they have said, "Yes" to yet another want.

Most quick-fix kids are talented at making 'wants' seem like 'needs'... just to be sure that parents will have no doubt that they are doing the right thing. Some children can make a 'want' plea sound like a 'need' plea. Quick-Fix parents have a hard time deciding if a computer or a TV is a 'want' or a 'need' in the kid's bedroom. A 'need' sustains life and relationships, love, affection, food, shelter, hugs, and so on. 'Wants' are desires such as for televisions, designer shoes and clothes, stereos, Maseratis, 3G iPhones, and so on. Children do not need 'wants.'

Wants

A want is for luxury items that are extras (toys, expensive electronics, designer anything, televisions in bedrooms, cars). Children do not need this stuff to have a good relationship with you. They don't need them to feel good about themselves. Allowing them to manipulate you into buying them sets up disrespect for you, a feeling of entitlement from them, and all around bad vibes. If they do receive these items, let them be as a result of their work and own earning power, or quite possibly a gift for a birthday or holiday if you feel so inclined and can afford it. Your kids will also have other wants that they are not ready to handle. They may want to start dating too early, want to stop piano or dance lessons too early, want to stop going to church. Quick-fix parents will let these kids stop these valuable activities because they don't want to force them into doing anything that makes them unhappy. Excessive giving of either material goods or freedoms does not create love, but rather dependency, entitlement and anger.

> "I hated piano lessons, just hated them, and I hated my teacher, Miss Arnold. She was a witch–really, really mean. I hated practicing too. My mom made me keep taking lessons, and I hated her for making me keep going. Finally, I got the nerve to tell mom how mean Miss Arnold was and we switched teachers, but I am so glad Mom made me keep taking lessons. So many people wish they had kept going with piano lessons, and I have never met anyone who regretted that their parents made them keep going. I appreciate my mom's caring enough to make me keep at it"

> "The Holly Hobby Birthday was a good example. I was so busy with graduate school

and looking back, realize how focused I was on school rather than the kids. I mean they were fed and clothed, and I paid attention and interacted, but my mind was always on what I had to do next for school. My younger daughter wanted a Holly Hobby doll for her birthday, so I bought her about five Holly Hobby dolls of varying sizes including the huge one, a full Holly Hobby Kitchen, and probably some furniture too. It was so excessive. It was an attempt to make up for time I wasn't spending with her, I wish I saw that then. She grew up expecting the American Dream, and those kinds of things I did created it."

Needs

A need is a necessity for the preservation of life. Children need shelter, water, food, and cleanliness. Their emotional needs include affiliation, encouragement, safety, trust, affection, honesty and authenticity.

Pack Leader Parents

Pack Leader parents are respectful to all groups of people and encourage their children to be the same. Although they don't agree with everyone and every lifestyle, they deeply respect the right of all people to hold the beliefs they do. Only God and maybe the Supreme Court can make decisions about what is right and what is wrong.

Pack Leader parents teach their kids deep respect for everyone. Naturally, as a healthy parent, you will have opinions, and can discuss, debate, and disagree and still have respect for those who disagree with you. Your opinion is your opinion only, it isn't the truth and you want your child to understand the difference.

So, express your opinions with humility, accepting that you know only what you know, and there may be much that you don't know. Pack leader parents teach their children how to develop their own opinions, how to weigh the pluses and minuses, how to look for evidence, and how to express themselves.

Because they see all people as equal, they teach their children to be accepting of others. Just because they love their children equally and teach their children to take care of others, inside and outside their families does not mean that they treat their children the same. Children are all different and require a different approach. You might be met with "it's not fair" when your children detect that you are giving more to one child than another, or that you are favoring one over the other. Take a good look at it, but if you are simply treating your children differently but equally, don't buy into the game, because it is just a manipulation!

6. Learn about
Discipline and Consequences

Pack Leader parents teach their children to manage life, within the rules of our society. When a child punches out another child, a quick-fix parent makes excuses for the child, or blames someone else. A Pack Leader parent considers it inappropriate, and disciplines the child.

> *"I felt like my dad thought I was so unique and special, I didn't need to follow the same rules as everyone else. Whenever I got into trouble at Little League, Dad would storm into see the coach and threaten him. In a twisted way, I got addicted to all the times that Dad would get mad at whoever was causing me problems. He never was with me otherwise, he was too busy. He always kind of threw out these sayings: "You're the best you know." "You're meant for something huge." I got into trouble with the law when I was about 18, and Dad was away then so I kind of cleaned it up myself. I haven't been in legal trouble since but I have never had a good relationship, and I just kind of feel detached from people. This stuff is really hard to undo, because it's kind of at the core of who I am."*

Most quick-fix parents believe that consequences for their children's acting out behavior will hurt their self-esteem. Their children will feel uncomfortable when they experience consequences, so this motivates quick-fix parents to stop consequences for their children. These children never learn to manage the natural, but painful emotions that come with life.

103

Pack Leader parents realize that children need to feel natural emotions, even painful ones, as a natural part of life. Natural emotions are emotions that are appropriate to the situation. If children experience a joyous event, the natural emotion would be joy. If they experience a loss, the natural emotion would be grief. If they experience a crisis, the natural emotion would be a crisis reaction. If they experience violence, the natural emotion would be a post-trauma reaction.

Be a pack leader. The following chapters explore the 5C's of pack leaders–compassion, clarity, consistency, commitment and confidence.

Chapter Six: The 5 C's

Effective influence is a sum of various factors. As a behaviorist (actions speak louder than words), I believe that change begins with action, then words, and finally beliefs. Beliefs are hard to change, unless actions and words change first. Practical, behavioral terms are central in communicating change.

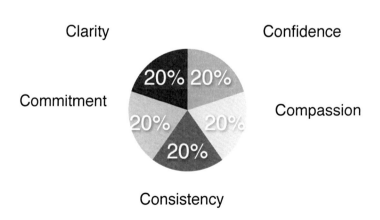

Each of these components is equally important; about 20% of the pie chart. It's hard to track all five, especially at first, but with practice you will be up to speed on all five areas, naturally and automatically. You will slip back into your old default mode when you are tired, or sick, or not being nurtured. When you do, you'll be gentle and patient with yourself, because you are always operating at the highest possible level. You will be able to recognize when you do slip back, and correct fairly quickly.

The Five C's of Pack Leadership:

1. Compassion:
> Do you care, is it about the other's good, are you seeing their part?

2. Confidence: Can you carry it off in a convincing way?

3. Clarity: Are you presenting it in such a way that others can hear?

4. Commitment: Do you really mean it? Does it line up with your true values?

5. Consistency: Are you following through? Are you requiring the same behaviors consistently, and are the consequences talked about in advance?

#1: Compassion

You might love the person who isn't 'listening' to you, but by the time you are reading this, I'll bet you're frustrated,

Compassion

annoyed, and do NOT see the other person's point of view. Why should you? It's not your problem. If only they would change, there wouldn't be a problem.

Ask yourself: do you really care about this person? If not, do you at least understand him or her? Is this issue for your convenience only, or there good for the other person as well? Are you really understanding their point of view?

People are more likely to listen to what you have to say and are more easily influenced if they sense that they have been heard and understood. Some actors, politicians, and sociopaths have mastered the art of faking sincerity, but most of us are not talented enough to be able to fake it. People sense when you genuinely don't care. So the first piece is compassion. Compassion means respecting and understanding, it doesn't mean agreeing. At least understanding the other person's point of view will go a long way to creating the relationship you are seeking.

**"It's easy to love the lovable.
The challenge is to love the unlovable."**

Get into Their World

To help shift their belief systems, get into their shoes and see the world the way they see it. Validate that it makes

sense to see it that way. Until someone else validates the way they see it, they cannot let it go. Whenever something doesn't make sense, that is, it is not validated, a person has to keep it until it does make sense. This is the basis of post-

Cartoon printed with permission.

trauma, everyday recollections, wake-up-at-3 a.m. experiences–you are trying to make sense or provide coherent explanation for something that's happening outside your range of understanding.

Clients would describe to me events from years ago, and the decisions that they made around those events. They had never told any one of these secrets, which they considered shameful, and the secrets interfered with their functioning.

> *"There was an old man who lived in the basement of the duplex apartment where I lived when I was growing up, say from about 3 until I was about 14. Everybody liked him and thought he was harmless, but I always felt creepy around him. I didn't what was wrong with me that I felt that way, since everyone said he was really innocent."*

When she was able to be validated that when she felt creepy, it meant that it was creepy, and someone should have intervened, she was able to let it go. There was nothing wrong with her that she had a creepy feeling when others felt that she shouldn't. She didn't have words to protect herself then, but she does now. I could intervene because I could help her understand her own logic, and because it made sense, she could let it go.

If there is a connection in the other person between their ideas and actions, you can persuade them.

Hostage takers are rational. So is your boss, and so is your teenager. The other side's position might not make sense from your point of view, but given their system of logic, their point of view makes perfect sense to them. It is your job to understand their belief system, their point of view and the actions or words that emanate from those.

What interests or beliefs lead him want to say no? When terrorists are motivated by public recognition for their cause, we tell them they have received radio and TV coverage, and if they kill the hostages they will lose face and be discredited. What is behind the other person's beliefs? With kids beyond age eight or nine, sit down and ask, "Okay tell me about why this is so important to you. There is something I am not getting."

Be likable.

It's hard to resist someone you like. If you want people to like you and do what you say, make them feel good about themselves when they're with you. People who feel good about themselves when they are with you, will more likely want to do what you say. If you are as frustrated as I sense you might be, think about how you've been acting. How cool it is to hang out with you? Do you make others feel great about themselves when they're with you? Do you listen to them so intently, with such focus, that they feel like the most special unique person in the world?

Do you focus only on the good in the person who isn't listening to you? I know it's hard. That doesn't matter. Your way doesn't work so well, this is a way that will work, so steam through it.

The highest form of love, in the Greek language, means "look for the good"

The highest form of love, in the Greek language[7], means "look for the good:. If you do love this person, you will look for the good in him or her, and give voice to it, *no matter what*. Let's assume we are talking about one of your children, and about praise. Here are some pointers:

Praise your child in specifics.

Praise successes. Feedback is most effective when it addresses the role that your child played in producing positive outcomes. For example, rather than saying "It's great that you got a good grade on your paper," bring up what the kid did, and one of his qualities (e.g. sticking it to it) by

by Mark Parisi

VERY GOOD! YOU STUCK YOUR END ON THE POT LIKE A BIG BOY!

RAINBOW TRAINING

offthemark.com
©2005 MARK PARISI DIST. BY UFS INC.

Cartoon printed with permission

---

7 Agape has been expounded on by many Christian writers in a specifically Christian context, but it is generally interpreted as "an intentional response to promote well-being when responding to that which has generated ill-being." It is one of several Greek words translated into English as love, and represents the divine, unconditional, self-sacrificing, active, volitional, and thoughtful love. Greek philosophers at the time of Plato have used forms of the word to denote an acceptance of the highest and most divine good in another. This love is in contrast to 'philia,' an affection that could denote brotherhood or friendship, and 'eros,' an affection of a sexual, or erotic nature. Agape is the highest form of love - the love of God would have for humanity.

saying "You worked hard on that paper, and you really deserve the good grade that you got." Then stop, because you will be tempted to say: "If you did that every time, you would be doing better in school." Don't say that, because it is a criticism and will cancel out your positive comment.

Praise efforts.

Research suggests that children who focus on improving their skills gain self-worth through growth. In contrast, children who only focus on achievements base their self-worth solely on their successes and failures. Praise efforts and improvement in skills, in addition to the praise directed towards their accomplishments.

Stop negative comments.

Research finds that praise and positive reinforcement are more effective in changing behavior, and sustaining positive behavior. Avoid making negative comments or giving negative feedback to a child. Instead, describe and praise what they should do, rather than what they should not do. We will work on the discipline part later.

Start today.

Make a list of 10 things your child does well.

1.

2.

3.

4.

5.

6.

7.

8.

9.

10.

Every day, choose one of these and say out of the blue: "You know Emily, I've been noticing how well you get up in the morning and get ready for school on your own. I really appreciate and value that."

Think about what she doesn't do so well, but is working hard to improve. "You know Emily, I've been noticing how much you are working on your cursive; I know that's important to you and I value and appreciate that."

P.S. This works with everybody.

Stop Judging
People will resist you (and not want to be around you) when you are judging them.

Old Judgment: "Look at those people lying around on the bench. Scum bags, why aren't they working?"

New Alternates: "They are Firefighters. Wealthy parents. Vacation. Recovering from breakdowns. Week to live, decided to relax.
Old Judgment: "You creep, you cut me off in traffic, and just sped away."

New Alternates: "Maybe his mother got in an accident. Late for work because helped person with flat. Spasm right foot. Practicing race car driver."

What is your reaction to these situations?

1. Your eight-year old tells you he and his friends were lighting matches in the neighbor's garage.
2. You're exhausted. You greet your spouse, who says, "I'm whipped, I've had a heck of a day."
3. You're the manager of a department whose company just announced new benefit package that you think is really good. Your direct reports tell you the one at other company is way better; and the one at your company is just hype.

What would you do in those three circumstances? Would you jump to conclusions? Would you judge? Or would you listen and show compassion, and learn more about what was happening in their worlds? Next time you have a chance, don't react. Stop. Just listen.

Next time you have a chance, don't react.
Stop. Just listen.

Hard to just listen isn't it! You want to just jump in there with your judgments and your advice. Shhh. Just listen to understand first, make sure you do understand, and then if you need to intervene, so be it.

Thomas Aquinas, who knew more about education and persuasion than many, once said that, *"If you want to convert someone to your view, go over to where he is standing, take him by the hand mentally and guide him. Don't stand across the room and yell at him, don't call him a dummy, don't order him to come over where you are. You start where he is, and move from that position."*

Involve the other person in the idea.
This could go under either Clarity or Compassion, and I put it here because it requires that you involve the other party in the request and decision, and is valid for folks in their teen years and beyond. Allow the other person to become involved in the idea so it becomes his. Involvement reduces resistance.

"Tell me I may listen. Teach me, I may remember.
Involve me, I will do it."

It sounds like:
"Building on your idea, what if we ..."

"So you're saying that ..."

"Something you said the other day prompted this ..."

"As a follow up to what you said earlier ..."

Satisfy unmet interests.

People never get enough of what they don't need. What they want never satisfies them.

Put yourself in his shoes; would you change if you didn't have to? What interests make him want to say no?

To the degree that you give others what they need, they will give you what you need. People never get enough of what they don't need. What they want never satisfies them.

We often assume resistance when we haven't yet asked clearly for what we need. You decide on the direction you need to take. Involve others in *how* this is going to happen. Here's an example with an adult relationship:

TAKE 1 (old way)

"Let's go to Pizza Nova for dinner. I love their pizza."

"Yeah, but the service is so slow."

"That's not true, maybe on busy times but it's always been good when I've gone."

"Listen, I've been there 4-5 times already, I know. Ask Jim, he's had the same thing."

TAKE 2 (new way)

"Let's go to Pizza Nova for dinner. I love their pizza."

"Yeah, but the service is so slow."

"Yeah, their service is probably slow at busy times.
>But they have really fresh stuff and I like the atmosphere."

"Maybe we could go early and try the service then."

Do you see how agreeing with their right to think and feel the way they do solves so many problems? Let other people be right too, for heaven's sake. Supposing you are shopping for an EveryReady™ battery, and at the checkout desk you say you love the commercial with the duck that keeps on quacking. The clerk says, "Oh that's not a duck, that's a rabbit." Enough said.

We all need to be right, and in relationships it's not a contest–both can be right. If you prove your husband or boss or child wrong, there's shame transferred, and it'll pop up somewhere later, even stronger. Next week, you will hear something like: "Oh I'm sorry, hon, I forgot to pick up the dinners for tonight. Heck here it is 6:55 p.m. and they'll be here at 7:00 p.m., Darn." Let people be right. Do not transfer shame, it will always return to you. Guilt and shame are like vapors, they linger.

Stop correcting others. If you are always in correcting mode, people will feel badly about themselves when they are with you–like lying in poison ivy, massaging a cactus

117

or drinking arsenic–they just will not want to agree with anything you ask. They will be too busy trying to get away from you.

The phrases below reflect Compassion. Read them through, and then check out the sample dialogue:

"That makes sense." "If I were you, I might feel that way." "Let's look at it like this." "That comes up sometimes when this happens." "I hadn't thought of that." "Let's consider it in just a minute, when we're finished on this area."

Take One or Take Two:
Which would you prefer to hear?

Them: "I can't believe you're doing this. I don't believe you. I have been planning this for months, it's all paid for, everybody else in the whole school is going, and I'm the only one not able to go because I didn't clean up my room. You are so screwed up. You are such a screwed up parent I can't believe it. I'm going outside."

You (Take 1): "You get back in here. Where do you think you are going? Who do you think you are acting like that around here? Just get back in here this minute, get into your room and clean it up. Don't you look at me that way, smart-ass. Get in your room and stay there. Don't bother coming out for *Gossip Girl* either."

You (Take 2): "Really disappointing isn't it?"

Them: "It's too much money."

You (Take 1): "Oh not really, you can pay for it over a year."

You (Take 2): "Yeah, it seems like a lot."

Them: "I hate my teacher."

You (Take 1): "That's not nice, Jennifer. She's only trying to help you learn."

You (Take 2): "What about her do you hate?"

Them: "I don't want to go out with him. He always makes these cracks about my weight."

You (Take 1): "C'mon lighten up, he's just kidding. You're too sensitive."

You (Take 2): "I don't blame you, I'd probably feel the same way."

B.C. Forbes: "No human being can be genuinely happy unless he or she stands well in the esteem of fellow mortals. He who would deal successfully with us must never forget that we possess and are possessed by this ego. A word of appreciation often can accomplish what nothing else could accomplish."

"Rings and jewels are not gifts, but apologies for gifts.
The only gift is a portion of thyself."
Ralph Waldo Emerson

calm
down.

smile.

listen.

Chapter Seven:
Confidence and Clarity

#2 Confidence

This section of the chart is about mastering the assertive energy of all pack leaders, with emotions and intentions that are lined up. Not so easy to do when you feel that somebody is driving you nuts. The very acknowledgement that somebody is making you feel a certain way indicates your belief that someone else can control your thoughts and feelings. If you believe that, then there is no way you're going to be able to pull off the calm assertive thing.

Stop saying, "she annoys me", "they drive me nuts", "he is inconsiderate", "she is making me crazy", "these kids

are driving me insane". They are not making you anything. You are choosing to be upset, or powerless, or act like a crazy person, because you either don't know any better or because it is helping you get your way. You could go on disagreeing with this, and keep holding the other person accountable for your life and well-being. But

it will never get better if you do; you're trying
wrong thing. You're pulling the wrong handle.

OK, accept that it is your response that isn't working.
This is what to start saying: "What she is doing is
triggering a response in me that is not working. My job is
to change my reaction, get calm, find grown-up words to
say, and get back in control."

If you have compassion and commitment lined up, even
though your confidence level is not a full 100%, you will
get it across. It is perfectly OK to admit that you are not
100% confident; in fact, it's a good idea to do so. With
your spouse, co-worker, or friend, and with a child who is
old enough to hear, you might say: "I am completely sure
of what I am saying, and I absolutely need you to listen to
it, but because it is new for me I am not that skilled at it
yet. Bear with me." Soon, you will master the pack
leader's calm and assertive approach. Like animals, others
sense our level of confidence easily, even though we think
we are good at acting the part. The old saying that, "a
river will never rise higher than its source" indicates that
your results will not rise higher than your belief in
yourself. This section is central to developing confidence:
first, figure out who you are.

Develop an Identity

What are your core beliefs? Take the time to think about how you feel about controversial topics. If you don't have strong opinions about controversial topics, then your identity might need work. When asked about controversial topics, do you feel swayed toward whomever is dominating the conversation?

Parents, without strong identities, have a hard time helping their children create their own identities, because children model their parents; if parents have little identity to model, there just isn't enough there. When parents don't understand their purpose, or direction, they can't feel their identity.

To create an identity (yikes what a huge topic), start with figuring out your values. What are they? Can you develop values that you hold as consistent? Parents with inconsistent values create confusion not only for themselves, but for their children. If you don't want your child to steal, but you cheat on your taxes, it's confusing. If your dad is hospitalized for a psychiatric illness and you hear that he is traveling on business, it's confusing. What if Grandpa is dead, but you hear that he is sleeping? Consistent values help create healthy kids.

Create consistency in your emotions, thoughts, actions, and relationships; they will help you get more stable and predictable. Tell the truth. People who hide and make up stories about their lives can't possibly own an identity ... because it's always changing.

So, create an identity by figuring out how you really feel about issues around you, and tell the truth in everything that you say and do. That's a huge order and will keep you plenty busy. The section on Clarity will help give you new words; this section will work on how you come off.

Communicate Confidence

Para-verbal communication refers to the messages that we send through the tone, pitch, and pacing of our voices. It is how we say something, not what we say. Para-verbal message accounts for approximately 38% of what is communicated. The only way you'll be able to work on this is to tape record yourself interacting with your child, or asking a supportive friend to monitor your tone and give you feedback. You'll hate it, but you don't hear yourself as you sound to others.

Nonverbal communication accounts for the other 25% or so (nobody has exact percentages and it doesn't matter). There are so many good books and courses on this topic; just consider this a primer.

1. Make eye contact.

Your eyes are your most powerful tool. Pack leaders expect their followers to maintain eye contact.

2. Check your posture.

 Many women slump to reduce their pectoral expansion. To practice, stand aligned against an outer corner with the top of your neck touching the corner. It will feel as though you are sticking your chest out; you aren't. You are in a position that conveys power and position. That's a good thing. Stand on two feet, stop shifting your weight from one side to the other. Keep your shoulders down; hunched shoulders show fear.

3. Use whatever natural gestures you want

Use any gesture except those that convey loss of emotional control (finger pointing, banging fist, finger drumming, change jingling, foot tapping). Those won't encourage others to listen to you.

4. Speak clearly, not too fast.

Don't yell, it only sounds like you've lost control (which you have). If you start yelling, stop and do a retake.

5. Keep a neutral, slightly positive face.

Frowning and looking surly in an attempt to look powerful do the opposite; you look out of emotional control (which you are). Don't smile if you are not feeling smiley.

Other Stuff:

1. Flashing or rolling eyes

2. Arms crossed, legs crossed

3. Gestures made with exasperation

4. Slouching, hunching over

5. Doodling

6. Staring at people or avoiding eye contact

7. Excessive fidgeting

8. Sighing, moaning

This is what you can ask that the other person do when you are speaking, and what you can expect of yourself when he or she has the floor):

1. Stay awake (not joking).

2. Look at the speaker, face the other person squarely.

3. Keep an open posture, arms and legs uncrossed.

4. Keep a distance between a half meter and two meters.

5. Respond to the speaker, i.e. nod your head.

#3 Clarity

Are you speaking in such a way that others can hear, or are you using words and phrases that tend to shut others off? If you still don't get that you are responsible for changing the system you're in, you'll still be annoyed that you need to listen to all this.

Are your requests direct and clear, or are they free-floating "we need-to ... somebody has to ... why don't you ... ?" Sometimes, when we think others aren't listening to us, it turns out that we've never made a direct request, and so our request has never been heard.

Sometimes when people resist, they just need more time to think about it. It helps to plan when you ask for things; don't wait until the last minute, when you're all tense and preoccupied.

> *"My older daughter said no to everything I asked her. I would get hysterical. She would always come around in about half hour, but we got into it several times before I caught on. When she was young she was always forced to hurry up, so she hated being trapped and put on the spot. So I said, hey think about this for a bit, and when you're ready, go downstairs and hang up your jacket and put away your boots."*

Work around the problem, instead of solving it. Every problem doesn't have to be solved. Every battle doesn't have to be won. The timing of putting the boots away wasn't that important; just that she did it. The mom described in the last chapter showed compassion (saw it from the daughter's point-of-view), and was clear as well.

Stop the following because they aren't working:

1. Attacking
... or interrogating ... criticizing ... blaming ... shaming

"So if your sales goals were higher, you wouldn't be in this situation would you?"

"Have you followed through with the gas company the way I asked you to do?

"Have you taken Jenny to the coach's for her soccer shirt?

"Did you call for a pickup for the airport tomorrow? Did you?"

"Have you found out if we're eligible for the Mills Act?"

"Obviously what you're doing isn't working. Anyone can see that."

2. "You" Messages
... or moralizing ... preaching ... diagnosing

How many times during the day do *you* hear:
"You'll have to get in the other line."

"You'll need to sign the forms by Monday."

129

"You'll have to call back Tuesday."

"You'll need to ask."

"You'll have to get permission."

How do you feel when people talk to you like that? Probably irritated and resistant. You wouldn't listen to them if you didn't have to; and others won't listen to you if you are in attack mode. People don't like to be told they need to or have to do anything.

"You don't seem to understand how important it is for Mike to get help. Don't you see that he's a sociopath?"

"You obviously don't realize that if you spent more time with her, we wouldn't be having this problem. You care more about yourself and your golf than you do your own children."

3. Getting into Power

... ordering... threatening ... commanding ... directing

"You do it this minute because I tell you, and I am your
          father."

"If you don't stop it this minute, it's all over for you."

(Swearing, name-calling, cold silence are all power struggle actions, and don't work).

How to Listen

You just want to scream, but you're supposed to listen. OK–big breath, calm down, and do what we talked about in the Compassion section earlier. See it from the other's point of view even if it kills you. You know this stuff, but you need to do it if you know it, to show that you know it. Otherwise you don't really know it.

Part of clarity–of getting messages straight–is listening. It's a combo of hearing what's said, and psychological involvement with the person who's saying it. Listening requires more than hearing words, as in "Shut up, I heard you, already". It requires really wanting to understand that other human being, small or big; respect, acceptance, and a willingness to see things from another's point of view.

Listening takes concentration and energy.

You're tired, I know, but you have to set aside your own agenda, put yourself in another's shoes, and see the world through that person's eyes. Real listening means to suspend judgment, evaluation, and approval so you can understand another's frame of reference, emotions, and attitudes. Listening is hard.

Batteries low

Self-centered people don't do very well at it, so if you are a poor listener you might be too self-focused and you might want to work on that.

If you're listening to someone, it doesn't mean that you're agreeing with him, just like if you forgive somebody, it doesn't mean that what he did was OK. It just means you're getting out of yourself long enough to allow a human connection. When you listen, you get good information you'll need to solve the problem, and a better understanding of the other person's truth.

Listening
1. Takes concentration and energy
2. Involves a connection with the person speaking
3. Needs willingness to try to see from another's truth
4. Requires that you suspend judgment and evaluation

> *"Listening in dialogue is listening more to meaning than to words . . . In true listening, we reach behind the words, see through them, to find the person who is being revealed. Listening is a search to find the treasure of the true person as revealed verbally and nonverbally. There is the semantic problem, of course. The words bear a different connotation for you than they do for me. Consequently, I can never tell you what you said, but only what I heard. I will have to rephrase what you have said, and check it out with you to make sure that what left your mind and heart arrived in*

my mind and heart intact and without distortion."
                    John Powell, theologian

Learning to be an effective listener is hard for many people, but the behaviors can be learned.

These are key Listening Skills to practice:

a. Restate. Reflect back what you thought you heard. When you do that, the other person feels heard and acknowledged, and that's a good thing, and we can be corrected if we heard it wrong. Instead of "What the hell now?" or "You want to do WHAT?" try:

"So you believe that we need to spend more time together without the kids."

"You want to go out Friday night and stay out until 10:00PM."

"You want me to come to the parent's night."

b. Reflect (the compassion, or empathy part of it)

Ask yourself, "How would I be feeling if I was having that experience?"

"You want more time with me, maybe you feel I am spending more time on the kids or other things than with you?"

"You want to be part of the group that stays out later."

"Sometimes you feel that I don't care very much when you see the other parents at parent's night and I don't go."

c. Question. Ask open-ended questions (that can't be answered with a "yes" or a "no") to get more information: "Can you tell us more about that?" "How was it?" "What does that feel like?"

How to Correct Behavior

In the Gottman et al. book *Meta-Emotion: How Families Communicate Emotionally*, the authors discuss Haim Ginott's basic plan for positive reinforcement. The four basic parts are:

1. Recognize and acknowledge the child's wish.
2. State the limit calmly and clearly.
3. Point out ways that her wish may be partially fulfilled.
4. Help the child express the resentment that arises when limits are imposed as in "I know you would like to watch the TV show now, but we will tape it and you can watch it after your homework."

1.	I can see that you want to stay later.
2.	We agreed on 8:00 p.m. and need to stick to that.
3.	Perhaps Joanie can visit at our place tomorrow.
4.	You will probably be upset with this, that's understandable.

1.	Yes, I hear you want to watch the next program.
2.	It isn't one that's OK to watch.

3.   You will be able to watch it when you are older, say 13 or 14. For now, you can watch your favorites, the ones we've agreed on.

4.   It might be frustrating not to be able to watch and you might not understand why, but there is content in there that it is better for you to hear. For that reason, you won't be watching it.

Here is more language for correcting behavior:

1.   When you throw your glass (describe)
2.   It breaks things (explain why it's important)
3.   That is not OK, and can't happen (consequence)
4.   So, when you are mad, instead of throwing your glass, use words to say you are angry and say what you want. Then I won't need to cancel your friend's visit. (what needs to happen).

(By the way, you had already decided together that throwing things meant no friends could come over on that day, and you're just sticking to it).

Rewards

Reinforcers vary from child to child. You know your child. If you don't know, find out the reinforcers that your child values, and use them: extra TV time, X-Box privileges, a Saturday at a shopping center, a show, time with friends–most kids enjoy these things. Use rewards when you feel your child has finished something difficult and something that is on your list. Don't confuse rewards with bribes. Don't offer extra treats, money, or gifts for

135

jobs you expect your child to do on a daily basis ... every pack member is expected to work for food.

Punishment

Since leaders never hit or strike, that action is out. Yelling means a loss of control, so don't yell. So what to do? See 'The Difference between Discipline and Punishment' elsewhere in this book. The most effective punishments are something aversive enough that they correct behavior. In an ideal, magical world, you would never use them; you would use only positive reinforcement to increase desired behaviors. It's not that perfect world, so you will need to either withdraw a desired thing or increase an aversive thing (stay later, more chores, no TV, etc). Just make it reliable and predictable, delivered without anger in a system that is orderly and in control; a system that you have set up in advance and that is agreed upon.

"Children have never been very good at listening to their elders, but they have never failed to imitate them."
James Baldwin

By being positive with your child and reinforcing the behavior you want repeated, you give her the blueprint for interacting with people outside your home.

How to be Clear

1. Speak clearly, firmly, slowly. Be specific.

No: "This room is a mess."

Yes: "Pick up your clothes and hang them up."

No: "I never get any help around here."

Yes: "Please help me do the dishes after supper tonight, and I would like the three of you to do dishes every night after tonight. I will show you how tonight and then it's your turn. You can divide it up any way you want."

No: "Would you mind picking up my cleaning?"

Yes: "Will you please pick up my cleaning?"

No: "What do you think of going out tonight?"

Yes: "I'd like to go to a show tonight. Would you like to go with me?"

Ask! A top real estate agent liked cigars, so sat outside chomping while people inspected homes. He didn't even wander through the home pointing out all the usual sales features; he figured people weren't stupid, they could see them for themselves. When they emerged, he asked them how they liked it. Then he said something that other agents didn't: "Why don't you buy it?"

"Would you like to book rooms with us? I am competing with the other salespeople to book the most rooms. If I do, I can take my children to the East coast to see their grandmother. Will you please book your rooms with us so we can go east?"

"Hi. My name is Jose Delgado. I deliver the *Union-Tribune* and give the best service in town. Will you please subscribe to the paper?

If you need to repeat instructions, directions or request, remember that people, especially young ones, need to be told things over and over. If you have to repeat a direction, say it as if it were the first time, don't get exasperated (that's out of control). Don't yell.

2. Be simple. Dumb it down.

by Mark Parisi

GOOD NIGHT... SLEEP TIGHT... DON'T LET THE BEDBUGS GNAW OFF BOTH ARMS AND BORE A HOLE THROUGH YOUR SKULL...

SLEEP CAME EASIER FOR DEWEY BEFORE HIS MOTHER TOOK THAT CREATIVE WRITING CLASS

offthemark.com

Cartoon printed with permission

Years ago, orders were passed down in fewer than five or six words, or with a simple visual signal. Dog trainers rely on short succinct consistent commands with hand signals. What's the length of the lecture you give your 14-year-old on

the state of his bedroom? How long are your memos?
Keep commands to five or six words. Use a visual signal
if one works.

Make a really short list of jobs, not a complex one you
found online in a parenting website. Employers make
their to-do lists so complex that it's too overwhelming and
impossible to track and reinforce. Simple lists (either
words or pictures) are better than simply telling your child
what to do. Some kids don't process multiple requests
quickly or accurately. Get your child's attention first. Use
a style described under Confidence and Compassion. One
thing at a time.

3. Ask in the positive future.

Instead of "You need to, you have to, you ought to, must,
say, "I would like you to."

Don't ask people why they do what they do.

People don't know why they do what they do. If they did,
they wouldn't want to admit it.

"Why do you act like that?"

"Why do you say those things?"

"Why do you want the same thing for dinner all the
          time?"

"Why don't you change your shirt at least?"

"Your teacher says you have so much potential, why
          aren't you using it?"

139

Avoid trap questions

"If I could show you how to save money, would you be
         interested?"
"You want to grow up strong and healthy don't you?"
"You feel responsibility and concern for your family,
         don't you?"
"Don't you want to be a good little girl?"

You want something from somebody else, and get
frustrated when you don't get it. What happens is that you
punish the other person–exactly what the other person
doesn't want–in an effort to get what you want. If the
other person is not strong enough to change, which is
most likely the case, help boost his self-esteem so he can.
Think of self-esteem as a jar of jellybeans. People have to
give some jellybeans away when they change. If don't
have enough beans, they will refuse, usually at the
unconscious level.

Ask for Help. Almost without exception, even young
children respond to a request for help. It is especially
powerful with adults. "I need your help." "Please help
me." "I have a problem, maybe you can help me."

Be clear.

Chapter Eight: Commitment and Consistency

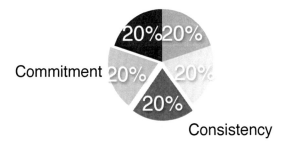

Commitment

Consistency

#4 Commitment:

Do you really mean it? How important is this to you? Is it in line with your values, and so deeply held, that you will not waiver, no matter what? For example, you want your children to eat vegetables–and you do believe in a healthy diet–but if you looked through your own food intake, is it more like lattes and bagels?

You have commitments, but without a commitment to your commitments, your requests will be shallow and unbelievable.

Get Real. Commit to your Commitments.
Believe it and Do it Yourself.

Don't lie, fudge or hide. People (especially employees, teenagers and animals) can see right through it. Want your employees to come in on time? Not waste time? Make more sales calls? Kids to not smoke or drink? Or not lie?

1. Deliberately create, and keep, small commitments.

If you are not committed to what you are asking of others, your credibility will be too low to expect anyone to listen to you.

Yoda says: "There is no try or no should. There is only do, or not do." Start by making a

list of your most important commitments, and rank them from most important to least important. Start with the top five in your rankings, and examine what your real commitment is, by examining how much time and money you spend on these commitments. If you spend close to none, get them off your commitment list, because you only wish you were committed to them, and you aren't. If you were committed, you would be taking action toward them.

by Mark Parisi

Cartoon printed with permission.

COMMITMENT	TIME	MONEY
Physical fitness		
Financial freedom		
Make more friends		
Be a better mother		
Develop artistic talent		

Chose which commitments you want to keep, and keep them. Put them on your to-do list, and work toward them

143

every day. There is a commitment list in the Appendix on page 184 you can copy and use.

If you have a top priority must-do, choose it from your list. Make sure it is concrete, such as "finish a book" rather than "encourage world peace." Since we are focusing on only one, decide again if you really want it. If you do, you will complete it. If you are not sure, or if you kind of want it, or if you are not willing to stop other activities for a while until it is done, decide not to do it now. Just get it off your plate.

by Mark Parisi

DAM! DAM! DAM! THIS IS OUR DAM HOUSE! I LIVE IN THIS DAM HOUSE! DAM! DAM! DAM!

TECHNICALLY, WE CAN'T DISCIPLINE HER... SHE DISCOVERED THE LOOPHOLE...

ATLANTIC FEATURE © 1995 MARK PARISI   offthemark.com

Cartoon printed with permission

2. Create a goal, and multiple sub-goals and steps under each sub-goal for your top commitment.

Make a detailed list and follow your plan. A tough part of accomplishing difficult or complex goals is the matter of delaying gratification. The long process can become discouraging without intermediate signals that you're on the right path–signs to encourage you. Set some of these intermediate goals up for yourself.

3. Once you are clear that you can commit to your own commitments, you are ready to commit to the system that you are designing for your pack member.

#5 Consistency

Since that fateful day when my Golden Retriever, Strider, discovered his first human food (a piece of hot dog) at the hands of a well-meaning stranger, he has been relentless

 in his pursuit of more. Because it hasn't been reinforced since then, the strength of his pursuit has been weakened over time, but has it gone away or been "extinguished"? No, nor will it ever. One shot, they've got you. One lapse, one screw up, just once you let them off the hook, just once you say yes when you should have said no, just once, they will be after you until you give in again.

If you are reading this book, chances are you've given in some time in the past, and been less than consistent. That's OK, it was what it was, and now it's water under

the bridge. It just means that you'll need to fortify yourself against the repeated attempts and manipulations that it's just natural for your child (or employee, or dog) to make. Just as surely as my dog remembers and will keep trying, on the off chance he'll get more food, your teen (or coworker, or friend) will keep trying, on the off chance that you'll break down.

Consistency. Do you change your mind, suffer lapses of varying degrees, or do you require the same behaviors every time? Can people around you predict with about 100% accuracy that you will always require the same behaviors, or are you running at about 50%? If you run at about 50% consistency, and those around you have any manipulative skill at all, chances are you are being manipulated most of the time, and your resulting resentment level is high.

If you have figured out your commitments from the previous section, and are really committed to what you say you are, then it's a simple matter of doing it repeatedly, no matter what (repeated from Quick-Start):

"But I'll have no friends"
"That might be true, but you won't be going tonight."

"But I'll fail in school if I don't go!"
"That might be true, but you won't be going tonight."

"You are so mean!"

"That might be true, but you won't be going tonight."

"I hate you so much!"

"That might be true, but you won't be going tonight."

"You bitch!" (slam door)
Silence. Smile, good for you. You're doing fine.

Don't make promises you can't keep and don't make threats in anger that you will regret later. It's tempting to

by Mark Parisi

IF YOU DON'T CLEAN YOUR ROOM, I'LL THROW AWAY ALL YOUR TOYS AND CANCEL THE TRIP TO DISNEYWORLD!!

EMPTY THREAT LEVEL

SEVERE
HIGH
ELEVATED
GUARDED
LOW

©2008 MARK PARISI DIST. BY UFS INC. offthemark.com

Cartoon printed with permission

147

make false promises and empty reassurances, and make commitments you can't keep. It's a quick-fix. Don't tell employees their jobs are safe or budgets are fixed if you don't know. Don't tell your daughter you will pay for her trip to Europe if you can't, even if you would like to. Promise only what you personally can deliver.

Manipulations

So you have said no, and you expect your child to listen to you. You are clear, calm and assertive. Your energy is good. You have examined why you are saying no, and you buy into it. You are prepared with consequences, and willing to commit to a long-term program.

by Mark Parisi
Cartoon printed with permission

Most quick-fix children realize that your first response of "No" is not your final answer. So with their usual, clever strategies, they whittle your firm "No" into a "Maybe" and eventually into a "Yes." They are so good at it. If it weren't so sad, you'd have to smile. Don't forget, they have strong feelings of entitlement, and they will actively work to persuade you to quick-fix them.

One of the strangest traps is this web of manipulation that your child will weave around you. If you are still not conscious of your own boundaries, or still need acceptance or approval from your child, you will fall prey. If you are working with someone who uses manipulation, (which will be virtually everyone reading this book who has someone who isn't listening) first read this note from a manipulator. It happens to be from a teenager with an eating disorder, but they all sound the same. It is the same system.

> *AN OPEN LETTER TO MY FAMILY*
> *I am a manipulator. I need your help. Don't lecture, blame, or scold me. You wouldn't be angry at me for having diabetes. Eating disorders, alcoholism, financial irresponsibility are diseases too. Don't hide my food; it's just a waste because I can always find ways of getting more. Don't let me provoke your blaming. If you attack me verbally or physically you will only confirm my bad opinion of myself. I hate myself enough.*
>
> *Don't let your love and anxiety for me lead you into doing what I ought to do to for myself. If you assume my responsibilities, you make my failure to assume them permanent. My sense of guilt will increase, and you will feel resentful. Don't accept my*

149

MANIPULATIONS

Sulking, whining, pouting

Being extremely hard working, or overly dedicated

Getting mad at you or accusing you

Calling you names

Telling you that you are mean and the worst parent ever

Saying, "I hate you"

Becoming helpless and confused

Blaming others

Pretending he doesn't care

Playing ignorant

Being passive: Silent or acting hurt or looking sad

Being extra agreeable and cooperative

Acting innocent

Giving you extra flattery or attention

"Promising" instead of "delivering"

"Trying" instead of "doing"

Withdrawing

Forgetting or being late

Being too busy or having no time

---

promises. I'll promise anything to get off the hook. But the nature of my illness prevents me from keeping my promises, even though I mean them at the time.

Don't believe everything I tell you; it may be a lie. Denial of reality is a symptom of my illness. Moreover, I'm likely to lose respect for those I can fool too easily.

Don't cover up for me or try in any way to spare me the consequences of my eating, starving, purging, drug binges, overspending. Don't lie to me, pay my bills, or meet my obligations. It may avert or reduce the very crisis that would prompt me to seek help.

I can continue to deny that I have a problem as long as you provide an automatic escape from the consequences of my behavior.

I love you.

Recognize that your child is functioning at the highest level possible he or she can, and is simply trying to get his or her needs met through unskilled quick-fix behavior. You caused this behavior. You and your child are responsible for maintaining it, and it is up to you both to change it. You alone are responsible for stopping the *conditions* that caused it. That is all you can do; you can't predict or control the outcome. You just have to believe that this system works, and trust it in faith. You have to keep your side of street absolutely clean, and know that eventually in his own time, he will too.

You will be neutralizing situations by not responding to them, you will not reinforce old quick-fix behaviors by enabling or rescuing them. Your new skilled responses will make the manipulation completely ineffective–maybe not the first time, or the 20th time, but eventually.

On the following page is a list of the traditional manipulations that you expect from your quick-fix child when you start to change. Manipulations are all designed to return you to the old system. Which ones your child uses will depend on your needs and vulnerabilities.

Guidelines on Handling Manipulations:

1. Don't get upset. It's not about you, don't take any of what he or she says personally. You might want to say to me: "Yeah right, this isn't your kid." OK, this will help: picture yourself as a lion or lioness, lying relaxed in the sun, licking your paws after a delicious meal of raw Wildebeest. There is a disgruntled hyena off in the edge of the clearing, jumping up and down in a tirade, furious that he didn't get enough food at this kill. She jumps, kicks, throws things, one of the branches even hits you. You understand her place in the jungle hierarchy, and are not upset. Mildly annoyed, but not upset. Only when she keeps at it, won't quit, throws a huge branch at you–do you swiftly rise, swipe at her with your paw and send her yelping. Then you settle back down in the sun. You, as the lion or lioness were super calm the whole time, just a swift paw, and it's all over.

Your paw use will be verbal (no hitting, ever). No need to get upset. Reestablish dominance and leadership with your own system of reinforcers.

Cartoon printed with permission

2. Don't reject the manipulator, it's not her fault. She is not bad, she has learned this is how she is supposed to be. If she is going to change, it will not be through lecturing or advice-giving. Faultfinding, moralizing, being a "psycho-pest" or leaving little dust-balls of negative energy around, increases resistance. Any change in your relationship can only be brought about by changing yourself.

3. Trust your gut, always. If you sense you are being manipulated, you probably are. Trust your intuition; your head is filled with bad advice that got you into this mess initially. If in doubt that you are being manipulated, buy time. Get help, ask for advice.

You: "You know what, I'm going to need some time on that one, I'll get back to you tomorrow morning."

Her: "But Mom, I need to know NOW. The kids are all sending in the money today and Mrs. Carlson said she needed a head count by tonight."

You: "I understand that Mrs. Carlson might need a head count tonight. It might help to call her and tell her you won't know either way until tomorrow morning, because I will let you know tomorrow morning."

Her: "I can't believe you. What is so hard about telling me whether I can go or not? I know, it's about the money isn't it? You never want to spend money on what I want, just what you want, like your Porsche."

You: "That might be, and I'll let you know tomorrow morning."

Her: "You are so mean."
You: Nothing.

Her: "I hate you!" (slams door and goes into room).
You: Nothing.

If you feel guilty, it means you are doing something right; you are breaking an old rule that no longer works. Good for you. Call your mentor, your support system, and check out your reasonableness. Don't do this alone. You cannot clearly see your own system, none of us can. You will walk a fine line between feeling selfish because you are withholding something you feel you should be giving, and feeling confident that you are doing the right thing. Guilt accompanies both sides, so they are tough to distinguish. You will be confused until you develop skills and the wisdom to know the difference between the two. Get someone on your side that you trust and bounce these things off them.

You will hear:	You will ask:
All, Every	Every? (every time, once?)
Never	Not even once?
Must, have to	What would happen if you didn't?
They think	Who's "They"?
Can't	What stops you?

Clean up all communications that potentially can block you from consistency and commitment. Get support; you don't need to do this alone. If you feel guilty, it's a good sign.

Chapter Nine: Acting Out

What happens when pack followers are missing a pack leader and attempt leadership themselves?

1. Back-Talk

There is a point where self-expression becomes harmful.

Back-talk crosses that limit. Kids who back talk want power–it's a basic control gesture and an attempt at pack leadership, that's all. Quick-Fix parents give in to back-talking children, which gives children more power. The

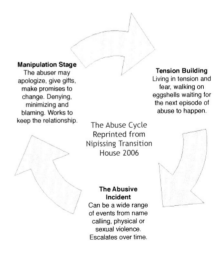

Manipulation Stage
The abuser may apologize, give gifts, make promises to change. Denying, minimizing and blaming. Works to keep the relationship.

Tension Building
Living in tension and fear, walking on eggshells waiting for the next episode of abuse to happen.

The Abuse Cycle
Reprinted from
Nipissing Transition
House 2006

The Abusive Incident
Can be a wide range of events from name calling, physical or sexual violence. Escalates over time.

cycle grows. Back-talking pushes parents' control buttons, igniting and explosion in parents. After the tirade, quick-fix parents feel guilty, which leads them to even more quick-fixes that gives them temporary relief. The cycle is as addictive as any other abuse cycle.

by Mark Parisi

THE PROBLEM WITH RAISING A SUN.

offthemark.com

Cartoon printed with permission

Responses other than exploding are to back down completely and give the child whatever he or she wants to avoid the back-talk. Some parents go overboard, and increase the pampering of their kids to preclude any possibility of back talk. Outside the home, the child expects the same treatment from classmates, teachers, principals, grocery store workers and eventually spouses. Some of these (those from similar backgrounds) will buy into the system and the cycle will be perpetuated. Others will not buy in, and the child will clash with the authorities. That is good.

Why do parents have trouble controlling the back-talker? Quick-Fix parents often believe that their parents raised them poorly, and they set out to correct their own parents' mistakes. When these parents were children, and their parents restricted their freedom to speak ("children are to be seen and not heard") they will try to correct their parents' mistake by giving their children complete freedom to speak without restriction–including rudeness–creating a whole new set of mistakes.

Children are the ones in charge when they back-talk. To get what they want, they back-talk with the warning: "If you give me what I want, you will be a good parent and I will stop back-talking for a while." Once you figure out which of the quick-fixes you are using, you can replace it and practice the 5C's.

1. Stop your child from back-talking by ignoring the back-talk (don't let it work) and then exposing it using the Rumpelstiltskin approach–wherein by naming the problem removes it's power: "You are back-talking to get this car, and you won't get it that way." Then stick to your statement.

2. Teach kids how to get what they want by asking or by working for it. Say, "Back-talking won't be helping any longer. If you want something, sit down and ask me for it

directly, or we can set us a schedule where you can work for it."

> *Leona would always whine and whine when she was being ignored. It happened every time, when her older sister or younger brother were getting attention and she felt left out, she developed this high-pitched whine that drove me nuts. I would stop whatever I was doing and yell at Leona to stop the whining! Satisfied that her whining was successful, she did stop for a few minutes. Then because it was a perfect solution, she would begin again. It was so predictable I wondered how I could miss it.*

> *So practicing the 5 C's, I took Leona aside and confidentially told her that I noticed that when she wasn't getting attention, she would whine and it would work for a while but not for long. I suggested that asking for attention would work better and for longer periods. She bought into it, we had a shared secret and bonded on our mission. I asked her if I could tell her dad what her new strategy would be because otherwise he might miss it. She agreed. So we all got together and decided that when Leona was asking for attention, it was a valid and mature way of getting something and could be honored with "OK" or "Not right now but in a few minutes." When she would whine, we decided that no attention would be paid no matter how annoying. I was amazed at how fast this worked because it was so effective. A year later it is still working.*

If you have tried to correct your child's back-talking or whining or sulking or any other acting-out behavior, and you are failing, you sometimes have to wait for natural consequences. You should mention to your child that eventually the world won't let him get away with it, so he might as well stop now. At some point, a teacher, principal or coach will have a problem with the same behavior. Let the consequences fall as they will, and your prediction will have some weight. Let him suffer the full consequences of his back-talking. He can be kicked out of school, kicked off the team, suspended, whatever it takes. Grit your teeth and accept it.

Sulking, Nagging, and Whining

Most quick-fix parents are caring people, and will do anything to stop their children's unhappiness, and their children know it. Sulking is an effective manipulative tool children use to effect a whole range of positive reinforcement. "Give me what I want, now!"

Nagging and whining are effective tools children use to put the pressure on, to get their parents to give in to their demands. Nagging and whining are very good at wearing the unsuspecting parent down until that parent gives in. If it is ignored at first, it increases because, like winning a jackpot or the lottery, they know that it will pay off, they just never know when. Quick-Fix parents want their children to be happy. Sulking, Nagging, and Whining children are not happy.

Crying

Kids cry real tears when they're physical or emotional hurt; you will obviously pay attention to those tears, and you will probably already know how to tell the difference between real and fake tears. When crying is fake, there is a different agenda.

Crying buys into the Quick-Fix parents belief that kids must always be happy for them to be good parents. 'Unconditional love and freedom' to you, means children should get and do whatever they want.

Quick-fix parents move fast to shut off bad feelings in their kids. A sad look in a boy's eye, a pout on a little girls lips, a silent faraway look on a teen's face–every child has practiced a different gesture based on their trial and error discoveries of what works with their particular set of parents. They are good at it. Very good. These are "Happy Meals" and Disneyland parents, the dream of every Madison Avenue marketing executive.

Quick-Fix kids use crying to avoid consequences of their behaviors or to get out of the consequences that they've already received. It's effective, judging by how many adults I see still using the tactic. One woman told me she just spontaneously cried when she was in trouble or when she was caught doing something wrong, such as speeding.

162

She said that that behavior stopped abruptly when one Highway Patrol Officer said to her: "That doesn't work. Whether you're crying or not doesn't affect how fast you were going and the amount of fine you are going to pay. Many women use that strategy, and it doesn't work, it just messes up your mascara. So you might as well stop." She said that jolted her into seeing that she was unconsciously using a strategy that she had learned years before.

What makes you buy into crying? Your kids will be unhappy? Won't love you? They will tell others what a mean parent you are? If it's crying in public, one of the most popular venues, is it the social embarrassment you want to avoid by giving in? When your children are really crying, bond with them, love them, be with them. Don't try to make it go away with food, toys, promises. That encourages the use of fake crying when the opportunity arises, and gives the child a message that real emotions are something to be shoved aside quickly.

Pack Leader parents know that Happy Children are not necessarily Healthy Children. Healthy children are allowed to be sad, allowed to be angry, allowed to express the full range of emotions without intervention by quick-fix parents. Learn to feel and express those emotions yourself! If you can't feel or express them, chances are that you won't feel comfortable when your child does.

For fake crying, the intervention is similar to sulking and whining. If you do give in and buy your kids out of their emotions, it's not the end of the world. After all you've done it a thousand times. Just try again next time. You can even disclose your strategy to your child: "I am working hard at not responding to your fake crying. Sometimes I won't be good at it, but it's my goal. Let me know how I'm doing, OK?" Give hugs, give closeness, give simple togetherness ... that never hurts. Don't give in to buying stuff or giving privileges that are not earned.

Don't Quick-Fix Grief

Feeling numb and stunned are a natural part of the grief process. With a serious loss, such as the sudden death of a family member, feeling nothing for a short time is common. If adults are experiencing stronger emotional reactions, they might think something is wrong with them for not feeling more. They don't know that feeling numb is helping them get through it.

If you or your child are going through a grief reaction, and you don't seem to be reacting at first–just accept it, support and nourish yourselves. To your child, say something like "sometimes when these things happen we feel kind of shocked, so we don't feel anything at all. That is natural and normal." Then be present and available to them when they do want to connect with you about their emotions, or lack of them.

Anger is just a signal that there is a primary emotion that needs to be expressed, probably fear. Following trauma, children can feel helplessness. Because Quick-Fix Kids are not coached to deal with the underlying issue that has created the helplessness, they're left to draw their own conclusions about why they are angry or scared. Because the immature mind is unable to look beyond self for causation, the natural reaction is to blame self. This can happen to young adults as well, and to any age if left untreated.

> *"There was always a money issue between my parents. They didn't really talk about it openly, but I could feel this thick-as-ice tension whenever dad bought anything we couldn't afford. Dad would get really mad at Mom if she said anything, even hitting her a few times, so maybe that is why I felt I had to say something when dad bought this big stereo system. I was around eleven years old at the time. I forget exactly what I said about the stereo that night, but dad got so mad that he grabbed my mother and I around our necks, and held us down on the floor. I had a hard time breathing and thought I might die. Mom was yelling as best she could and I couldn't say anything, and after a while, he just let go and walked away. Mom went to her bedroom and I went to mine. I didn't cry, I just felt weird–we never talked about it, ever. That was many years ago, and throughout my adult life I have never let anyone touch my neck, and have always wore turtlenecks. I don't know, but it's amazing that just one episode that isn't talked about can cause all that!"*

After death or divorce, children naturally (and usually) want that parent back. It is tempting to quick-fix at this time to prevent uncomfortable emotions. Sometimes another relative will step in and assume the role, even allowing himself to be called Dad. When that happens without the emotional component of grief having been expressed, the child never learns to accept the reality of losing dad and to adjust to that reality.

Teasing and Bullying

Children try to achieve Pack Leader status by using teasing and bullying. It doesn't work, except in the vulnerable quick-fix family pack. Many parents view teasing and bullying positively; it proves that the child is dominant and strong and can fend for him or herself, or simply use the excuse of 'Boys will be boys'.

> *"Jim's dad is an ex-Marine and couldn't stand that Jim was gentle and non-combative. So he teased and bullied Jim, until Jim did get really upset with him. Jim is 18 now and is mad at his dad; I mean he is bonded at a level, but they are not that close. His encouragement of Jim's anger didn't work. By putting him down and teasing him, he only diminished his motivation."*

Where do they learn how to tease and bully?

Father: "Any more makeup you could work at the local
         whorehouse."
Teen daughter: "Daddy!"
Father: "Just kidding."

If you are teasing and bullying–stop! If you are tolerating teasing and bullying–stop! Your children are hurting others with teasing and bullying. Do you tease? Have you ever been teased? It is a devastating method of hurting another person because of the complete lack of accountability it affords the attacker. After a teasing episode, when the attacked tells the attacker of the hurt, the attacker simply replies: "I was just teasing."

Create consequences for both yourself (if you tease) and for your kids when they tease and bully.

Tantrums

> *"I always got into it when Melissa would just stop and drop whatever she was carrying and just scream, just scream. This little three-year-old blond haired lovely child turned into this red-faced monster and it would always be at Wal-Mart or in the drugstore or wherever."*

A tantrum is an often-effective one-person show designed to command an audience, and pulled off effectively with kids even younger than a year old. Tantrums are designed to buy into all the other quick-fix beliefs, along with

167

social embarrassment. They occur when they have the most likelihood of working; when parents are most vulnerable–in stores, churches, public meetings, when friends are over ... you think of your special times. Those are times when mom or dad will most likely buy in, and give whatever they need to quiet the child. The payoff will stop the tantrum, and is a powerful reinforcer for future tantrums.

The same quick-fix unconditional love belief that children should get whatever they want and do whatever they want, operates here too. Children have poorly developed mechanisms for delaying gratification. When they do not get what they want, they get frustrated. Quick-Fix parents try to get rid of their children's frustration, preventing them from learning skills. This is what Pack Leader interactions sound like:

Child: "I want some money."
Parent: "What job are you going to do for it?"

Teenager: "Can I borrow the car?"
Parent: "You can borrow it, if you wash it first."

Child: "Can my friend stay overnight?"
Parent: "Yes, if you clean your room."

Child: "I'm hungry!"

Parent: "Let's make supper together and do the
                     dishes together."

Pack members earn what they get, including food.
Children should earn most of what they want. When your
kids have tantrums when they want stuff for nothing, let
them be. Teach them how to earn what they want when
they are out of tantrum. Quick-fix parents really feel they
are withholding love when they say, "No." They often feel
so badly, that they need to explain to their children the
reasons for the "No", which they don't. Kids will learn to
ask "Why not?", and parents will struggle, and kids will
ask, and parents will struggle. "Because I'm the Mommy,
that's why." When children use tantrums to get what they
want, just answer "No", with no explanation.

Children use tantrums to push parents' buttons, so they
can get a new toy or expensive activity. Pack Leader
parents know their own buttons–this is part of knowing
their own identity. They can feel when their children have
pushed their buttons. When they feel their buttons pushed,
Pack Leader parents realize that their children are trying
to manipulate them.

Tantrums are children's way of saying that they don't
know how to get what they want, and that it is time to
teach their children some skills; to use a different set of
behaviors instead tantrums.

169

No advance credit! Never give children the privileges first, with the promise of work later. This is a huge quick-fix parent problem. When they have to wait, they are learning to delay gratification until they earn it. This is the way it is for adults. You work first, you buy later.

Scapegoating

Whoever is the scapegoat is given unjust blame for everything that goes wrong in their family. The advantages to scapegoating–one person is the scapegoat, the others are off the hook. Everyone else does not have to accept responsibility for family problems. A problem rarely exists at the level it is expressed. If one person is being blamed for the family problems, or being labeled as the black sheep, you are in the middle of a Quick Fix. This one needs professional counseling to get you out.

Lying

Exaggeration inflates self-esteem. Kids get the enthusiastic attention they crave. Exaggeration colors kids who feel like 'gray children'. Distortion requires children to be deceptive with hidden motives, such as setting up another child to take the blame for their misbehavior, denying the truth to get out of trouble, avoiding responsibility. Distorting, a form of lying, requires children to make a commitment to lying, to keep the original lie believable. With this advanced lying, children actively rehearse lying to others. So, they are making a greater commitment to lying and can become very accomplished liars, beginning to believe the lie themselves.

If your child is lying, go back to the other repairs we talked about such as listening and spending more time. A lying child has a serious system malfunction. If you are not sure, have him pass the *7-day Test* about the event of concern.

The 7-Day Test: Ask specific questions about the event. Listen to your children's answers. Then ask the same questions one week later. Truth is consistent, so their answers will not change if they are being honest.

If your child is caught lying outside the home, be grateful that natural consequences will be on your side Just do not rescue. A coach was about to kick a basketball player off the team because he was caught in the woman's dorm selling cocaine. He was obviously guilty, but his mother lied for him telling school officials that he was home with her on the night he was accused. They accepted her lie and he stayed on the team. Parents lying for their children damage the bond of trust and damages the character of the child. If the relationship is founded on dishonesty, real trust cannot grow.

Lying by omission is manipulative, and is still lying; kids selectively withhold important information from their parents. As adults, they won't feel as though they are lying, it has become such an integrated part of their character. Call it out, bring it to the surface.

Stealing

Young children occasionally take something that does not belong to them, and most parents do the traditional discipline of having their children apologize and make restitution. Persistent stealing as shoplifting is a serious legal and psychological issue. Why do they do this? For excitement, to create anger in parents, to call attention to issues in their family, because they feel entitled and justified when stealing–several reasons.

There are no excuses or blaming allowed with stealing as with lying. **Hold children accountable.**

Quick-Fix parents shield their children from the consequences of their own actions, as well as the complications of life. Even when security arrest a shoplifting quick-fix child, the child expects special privileges and becomes angry when they aren't received.

Entitlement knows no bounds. Many shoplifting kids do not believe the problem started with their decision to shoplift. The child usually blames the store owner, and blames the police, feeling it all unfair, and Quick-Fix parents will support the blaming.

Most children who shoplift have self-inflated egos (not a good thing—means low self-esteem), needing to believe they are much smarter than adults, believing they can outsmart anyone. They are surprised when they are arrested. Once children steal once, it is easier for them to steal the next time. If police arrest children for stealing, it is rarely the first theft.

Pack Leader parents have children confess, apologize, and make restitution. They take the appropriate legal consequences. They get family counseling.

Now what?

I know these things to be true:

Once more: reading this shows you care about making things better, improving and healing yourself not only for your current relationships but for the next generation.

No matter how bad things have become, they can always improve and be healed. That is a testimony to the power of the human spirit. Things don't get better on their own. Separating and giving distance won't make it better. It only makes it easier temporarily. The only way beyond it is through it. Winston Churchill once said, "If you're going through hell, keep going."

If you are resentful, it means that you have given up your own power and decision-making ability, given someone else responsibility for your life, and let him or do as they wish with you. You feel victimized and hurt, and are mad at the other person for treating you this way, and demand that he or she change to suit you, rather than speaking up and taking responsibility for yourself. This is a very immature way of handling life, one which you used years ago as a child when you had no choice. It no longer is working for you, and it is time to give it up, and grow up.

No matter how out of control things have become, none of it was your fault. You didn't know. You didn't ask to not know how to lead a pack. You didn't understand how to take power; you weren't shown how to do it. Now that you know what happened to you earlier on to create the current conditions, how to take charge, and what to do to move forward, it is your fault from now on if you don't change. Make the decision to change.

Find out what it is that you want, have the courage to put words to it, and make it happen in your life. Stop blaming others for how they are treating you, because they are treating you exactly the way you have asked to be treated by them.

There is nothing that you set your mind to that you cannot do. Speak up and take charge. You are the pack leader. They are waiting for you to lead and will feel very relieved when you do.

It might be helpful to copy the cut-outs on the following pages and carry them around with you while you are learning new behaviors. Hope they help. Good luck, and I believe in you.

APPENDIX

From *C.A.R.E.S. Companion Animal Resource & Education Society (Schenectady, NY) & Progressive Animal Welfare Society*
http://www.cbrrescue.org/articles/packleader.htm

Establishing Yourself as Pack Leader

Whether you have just adopted a young pup or an adult dog, you have many things to teach your new companion. You want your dog to be loved, trained and lively, but not spoiled, a robot or uncontrollable. Dogs can be naturals at learning manners and commands, particularly when you understand a key aspect of their nature. Dogs are social, pack-oriented animals. Your dog will respect a strong, clear, fair leader. If you fail to establish this position for yourself, your dog will feel obliged to try to take the position of leader for himself.

The Alpha Role

In a natural state, dogs would live their entire lives within the closely structure social order of their pack. While young, they would begin to learn the workings of the pack's social system and, as they grew, begin to establish their place within the pack's dominance hierarchy. Dominance, submissiveness, leadership, obeying others– these are all concepts that are understood by every dog. These are all concepts that you must understand as well if you are to relate you your dog in a successful manner.

Each pack has a leader, an individual who is dominant over all pack members. In wolf society, this individual is called the "alpha." This is the member who makes the decisions, who must be obeyed. This is the individual that you must be in your dog's eyes.

Steps to Establishing Your Role as Alpha

Professional trainers know that it is a waste of time to try to train a dog without first establishing themselves as alpha to the dog. Every dog needs a leader to listen to and adore. Without this leader, a dog will feel lost and unstructured. If you do not take the role of alpha, your dog will be forced to take the role himself. Here are some steps to establishing your role as the alpha. Notice that these involve both behavior and body language–two types of communication that your dog will understand.

1. Always praise your dog as if you own it. Put your hands firmly on the dog. Hug the dog. Pat him so that your hands get warm from the contact. Do not praise him in a timid way.

2. Praise warmly, well and quickly. Do not drag out your praising of a working dog. Do not fawn over the dog just because he did one sit-stay.

3. Reprimand fairly and quickly, then forgive. Don't hold a grudge. When you put your hands on your dog, do it with confidence and authority. Hands on does NOT mean hitting. Hands on may mean a collar shake, a leash correction, a surprising assist into a sit or down. Do it quickly and with authority. Then when you've made the dog do exactly what you want–once–give him a hug. That's alpha.

4. Make the dog obey on the first command. Don't get into the habit of repeating yourself. A dog's hearing is significantly better than yours, and you can bet he heard you the first time.

5. Give commands only if you can follow through, and make sure you always follow through. If the dog is running across the park to meet another dog, do not yell "Come!" because if he decides not to obey, you have no means of correcting him. Once he accepts you as leader, he will stop and return to you–because he will have learned that leaders are to be obeyed.

6. Give permission. Give it for what is about to do anyway as long as it is OK with you. This does not mean you say OK when you see your dog about to steal a plate of cookies. This means you do say OK when your dog is about to get into the car for a ride with you, eat the food in his bowl, go out with you for his afternoon walk. It means that in a subtle way you are teaching the dog to look to you for approval and permission instead of making decisions on his own. Remember - the better behaved the dog, the more freedom and fun he can have.

7. Deny permission. Monitor your dog's behavior. Teach him some manners. Even if you like him to walk on your couch and coffee table, he shouldn't behave that way in other people's homes. When you take him to the lake, he should wait for permission to swim. It may be too cold some days or there may be too many young children swimming.

8. Do a sit-stay. This is an easy way to reinforce your role as alpha. Put the dog in a sit-stay for five to ten minutes. For particularly dominant dogs, make it a down-stay, and even more submissive position. If he's a wild animal and he doesn't know the meaning of the word *obedient*, all the better. When he breaks–and he will–put him back. If he breaks 14 times put him back 14 times. At the end of a few minutes, the dog knows you're alpha. He knows that anyone who holds his leash can call the shots. And this is with no yelling, no hitting, no electronic stimulation, no leaving him in the kennel or garage for three days, no nothing. Just a sit-stay. Easy and effective.

9. Be benevolent, but tough. Act like a top dog. Tough, but loving. Always be fair and never get angry. Dogs understand what's fair and what's not.

10. Be a model to your dog. The top dog behaves with dignity, surety, confidence, authority, and intelligence. This will help your dog to be calm himself.

11. If you have more than one dog in your home, you decide the "pecking" order within the dog pack by routinely feeding the "top" dog first, giving that dog bones first, etc. Make the others wait for their turn. This is another means of exerting your authority.

Your Dog Will Be Happier

You may think that this system is just being too controlling and not "fair" to the dog. Actually, by being consistent in your handling and in your demands on the dog you are being fair. He needs structure–to understand what you want and what his responsibilities are. What is truly unfair is giving up a dog because of behavior problems–problems caused by the lack of structure and guidance that were the owners' responsibility to give. Unfortunately, animal shelters are filled every day with these dogs. Firm, loving training will keep you and your dog happy–and keep you together.

The Needs of Children

Brazelton and Greenspan, in *The Irreducible Needs of Children*, identify seven irreducible needs children have are:

1. Ongoing nurturing relationships. Both emotional and intellectual development depend on the security of having steady, warm relationships, not just educational games and cognitive stimulation. When relationships are not available because of distracted or inconsistent parenting, children are more likely to lack motivation.

2. Physical protection, safety, and regulation. Children need assurance that their physical and psychological being will be protected from harm, including protection from environmental toxins to psychological abuse.

3. Experiences tailored to their individual differences. The nature of each unique child be nurtured.

4. Experiences appropriate to their age. Too much or too little stimulation for the child's age level or stage of development can hinder development.

5. Structure and discipline. Adults need to set limits, and to empathize with the child and his or her weaknesses.

6. Stable, supportive communities and cultural continuity. A stable environment that provides a continuity of values from family, peers, and the community at large.

7. For the critical first three years of life are that each child have one or two steady primary caregivers; that working parents be available for at least two-thirds of the evening hours with the child; that no more than one-half hour per day be spent watching television; and that, in cases of divorce, the child not be separated from the primary caregiver overnight.

Pack Order Basics

★ Decide what rules or behaviors are important, those that won't budge.

★ Get everyone in the house on the same page about these.

★ Get clear and consistent about the rules. Kids can't read your mind.

★ Don't enforce rules when you're too angry or tired to think straight. Give a Calm Delay and wait until later.

★ Never yell or hit. These out-of-control behaviors put your child in power. If you do, apologize and get back on track.

★ Reward your child only when following the rules, and in a calm state. Think out rewards ahead, consulting with your child.

★ Spend time hanging out with your kids.

★ Tell the truth, no matter what.

★ Don't do anything for them that they can do for themselves.

★ Figure out your own identity, your goals and dreams.

★ Sort out the difference between Love and Permissiveness

★ Sort out the difference between Wants and Needs

185

It's Not About Me

I can stop trying to impress others. How others feel about themselves when they are with me determines how much they will like me.

Pack Leader
Calm-Assertive Energy

Stop saying powerless, ineffectual comments: "she annoys me" "they drive me nuts" "he is inconsiderate" "she is making me crazy"

They give power to the other person (not a leader position), feed into your victim status (not a leader position), and show resentment toward the other person (not a leader position).

My Reminders

Is what I'm sharing interesting, valuable, or important or useful to them (not me)?

Others will bond to me to the extent that I am listening to them. Am I really listening?

Am I announcing how I want people to react to me, by saying something like, "This is cool, listen up, you'll love this!"

Am I consistent or have I lost credibility?
To be credible, I will be consistent.

Get Real. Commit to Commitments. If I'm not really committed to the issues that I say I am, and I try to enforce them in other's lives, they just won't stick.

I don't need to be liked, but I do need to be respected.

It's not my fault. I did the best I could at the time with what I knew.

Keep my own side of the street clean. Take care of my own issues, let others take care of theirs.

My Choice

1. Change the other person
2. Change the situation
*3. Change myself

"God grant me the serenity to accept the things I cannot change, the courage to change the things I can, and the wisdom to know the difference."

Calm down. Be a relaxed, in-control and in-charge leader. People will feel better when they are around you.

Smile. Joy attracts joy.

Listen. It's not all about you. People will feel great about themselves when they are with you according to the quality of listening that you give them.

Trust me. Not because I'm a doctor, but because I learned the hard way.

COMMITMENT	TIME	MONEY

INDEX

THE AUTHOR

Dr Janet Lapp translates psychological theory into down-to-earth terms that people can readily use to make their lives better.

A former professor, researcher, clinician, and Registered Nurse, Janet was born and raised in Canada, and her PhD is from McGill University in Montreal. She is a licensed clinical psychologist, and creator and host of the award-winning CBS series 'Keep Well.' As editor of the *FastChange Letter* and author of three books: *Dancing with Tigers Plant your Feet Firmly in Mid-Air*, and *Positive Spin*™ she has received critical acclaim for her forward-looking ideas. Admitted into the Speakers Hall of Fame, the "Oscar" of Professional Speaking, one year she was rated by Toastmasters as one of the top three speakers worldwide.

Janet has two grown daughters, four grandchildren, learned the material in this book the hard way, and currently lives in San Diego California with her Golden Retriever, Aragorn (Strider).

Other Books and Things

Go to www.lapp.com
or email orders@lapp.com for more information

Books

Plant Your Feet Firmly in Mid-Air (Change Leadership)

Dancing with Tigers (Overcoming)

Positive Spin (Happiness and The American Dream)

Leading at the Edge of Change (High-Risk Leadership)

Audio

Make it Happen: 4 CD Taking Risks Program
          with pocket book: Make it Happen

Plant Your Feet Firmly in Mid-Air 4-CD Program
          (good accompaniment to book)

Miscellaneous

Decision Cards - Pack of 30 cards to help your team make
          better and faster decisions